Le

IM

SAINTS

Legends of the
IMPROBABLE
SAINTS

RICHARD COLES

Illustrated by Ted Harrison

DARTON·LONGMAN + TODD

First published in 2013 by
Darton, Longman and Todd Ltd
1 Spencer Court
140 – 142 Wandsworth High Street
London SW18 4JJ

ISBN: 978-0-232-53002-5

A catalogue record for this book is available from the British Library.

Text designed by Ted Harrison and Judy Linard

Printed and bound by Bell & Bain, Glasgow

INTRODUCTIONS

Following the mass conversions sweeping Britain last year after the publication of *Lives of the Improbable Saints*, Dr Harrison and I thought it wise and expedient to retell yet more stories of the great 'cloud of witnesses' preserved in Christian tradition these two thousand years.

The usual rules apply. I have tried to adapt ancient hagiographies to suit contemporary readers and have cheerfully suggested patronages where I think it appropriate; but I have not made any of them up even though this distasteful suspicion is harboured in the breasts of many of my readers, and the accusation is constantly flung at me via social media. I just think of St Sebastian and crack on.

Also, as the publication deadline approached, I'm afraid I got lost on the Mull of Kintyre when the camper van got a puncture so Dr Harrison kindly filled in some blanks by constructing a useful calendar of their various feasts and memorials, interpolating other significant events for context.

We do hope you enjoy them; and maybe even hear their distant triumph song as they go by.

RICHARD COLES

The illustrations stretch the bounds of visual plausibility to their utmost limits. No pious bishop or saintly sister is treated with respect. The cartoons even make light of hideous sufferings and tribulations. Little is historically correct. But an artist, it is said, should never apologise.

TED HARRISON

CONTENTS

St Felix of Nola

He was bishop's chaplain to Maximus around the time
of the Decian persecution in the year 250. The Roman
authorities came for the aged and feeble bishop but
he fled to the hills and Felix was taken in his place.
Horribly tortured, an angel came and released him from
prison and he went in search of Maximus. Eventually he
found him starving and suffering from exposure in the
mountains. Felix picked him up and carried him to an
old lady's house and nursed him back to health, but had
to flee again when the Roman soldiers came after them.
He then hid in a derelict building, but when a search
party arrived it looked like all was lost. Fortunately a
spider miraculously wove a web over the doorway to
where they were hidden and the soldiers, who were
all scared of spiders, turned away. Then Felix and
Maximus went to live in an old well until the all-clear.

St Sigfrid

Sweden's patron saint was, in fact, an Englishman, born in Northumberland in the tenth century and sent to Scandinavia as a missionary by King Ethelred the Unready. Hearing rumours of gorgeous robes and precious vessels used at the Mass, King Olaf of Sweden came to see Sigfrid and was so enchanted by his manners he accepted baptism in a magic spring. Sigfrid was assisted in his missionary work by his three nephews, Unaman, Sunaman, and Winaman, but while he was away they were attacked by some rascals and beheaded. Their severed heads were put in a box and thrown into a pond. Sigfrid miraculously recovered the three heads and asked the heads if the crime would be avenged. 'Yes,' replied the first head. 'When?' asked the second. 'In the third generation,' answered the third. And so it came to pass. Sigfrid, in spite of this, became an early advocate for the abolition of the death penalty.

St Hildegund

She was twelve when her mother died, and her father, Knight of Neuss, decided to take her with him on a crusade to cheer her up. Women were not allowed so he dressed her as a boy but on the way home he died at Tyre and Hildegund was robbed by the man he had paid to take care of her and left for dead. She recovered and still dressed as a boy made her way to Cologne where she became a servant of one of the canons of its cathedral. He decided to take her to see the Pope but Hildegund managed to get convicted of robbery and was condemned to death, despite surviving trial by red hot iron. She was hanged, but cut down in the nick of time and eventually ended up as a Cistercian monk at Schönau Abbey. Her true gender was only discovered after her death in 1188. She is the patron saint of trousers.

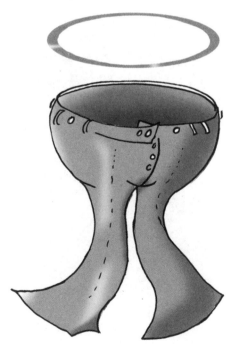

St Brychan ....

He was a fifth century Welsh king and patriach. He was the father of Cynog, Rhain Dremrudd, Clydwyn, Arthen, Papai, Dingad, Berwyn, Rhydog, Cynon, Pasgen, Cylflifer, Marthaerun, Rhun, Caian, Cynbryd, Cynfran, Cynin, Dogfan, Dyfnan, Dyfrig, Hychan, Llecheu, Neffei, Rhawin, Llofan, Llonio, Heilin, Afallach, Gwynnen, Gwynnws, Meleri, Hunydd, Ceingar, Tudglid, Nyfain, Gwawr, Marchell, Lluan,

.... and family

Gwrygon, Goddeu, Arianwen, Bethan, Ceinwen,
Cerddych, Clydai, Cynheiddon, Dwynwen, Eiliwedd,
Goleudydd, Gwen, Lludd, Tudful, Tudwystl, Tybie,
Beiol, Tydieu, Eufail, Hawystl, Edwen, Gwenrhiw,
Tudwen, Callwen, Gwenfyl, Gwennan, Mwynwen
and Gladys, but would not qualify for child benefit
because of his royal revenues. At least 24 of his children
themselves became saints.

St Joseph of Arimathea

According to legend he was a wealthy commodities trader and a kinsman of Jesus, who accompanied him as a boy on some trips to Cornwall, where he'd outsourced his tin production. This is the origin of Blake's poem 'Jerusalem' – 'and did those feet in ancient time?'. After Jesus' crucifixion and burial, in which Joseph played an important part, he returned to England with the Holy Grail, the cup used by Jesus at the Last Supper. On arrival at Glastonbury, he planted his staff in the ground and from it there sprang the Holy Thorn, which flowers to this day at Christmas, when a nosegay from it is sent to the Queen. In the Civil War a Roundhead tried to cut it down, but it shot thorns into his eyes and blinded him. Vandals, in recent years, have been more successful.

St Malo

The Feast of St Malo is 15 November. He was a Briton
who fell in with St Brendan the Navigator and set off on
a voyage during which they evangelised the Orkneys and
resurrected a dead giant called Maclovius
on the island of Cezembres. Once
raised, they baptised him and then
killed him again so he could go
to heaven. Malo ended up as
bishop of Aleth in Brittany
where he was terribly gentle
and sweet. One day, while
preaching, he spread
his cloak and when he
finished saw that a jenny
wren had laid her egg on
it. He sat down beside it
and waited for the eggs to
hatch and was untouched
by rain, a miracle. For
all his kindness he had
a terrible singing voice
and was driven away
by the people of Aleth
for a while, but they
let him come back.
He is patron of
swineherds.

St Cassian of Tangiers

He was the Exceptor at the law courts of Carthage responsible for recording the details of proceedings. One day the Centurion Marcellus, a Christian, was brought in on charges of treason. It was a show trial, presided over by Aurelius Agricola, the deputy prefect, who on scant evidence found Marcellus guilty and sentenced him to death. On hearing the sentence pronounced Cassian threw down his pen, refused to write any further and announced that he too had become a Christian. The deputy prefect had him arrested and summarily beheaded, recalled in Prudentius's long hymn of the martyrs, the Peristephanon: 'Ingeret Tingis sua Cassianum, festa Massylum monumenta regum, qui cinis gentes domitas coegit, ad iuga Christi.' He is patron saint of stenographers.

St Eusebius of Mount Coryphe

A Syrian monk who was renowned for his austerities, praying continually and eating only once every four days. One day listening to his abbot read from the Scriptures, he allowed his attention to wander and dwell momentarily on thoughts unbecoming a celibate and a solitary. As a punishment he had a blacksmith forge a heavy iron collar connected to an iron girdle contraption and 'chained his neck to his girdle that he might be compelled to violate the prerogative of his manhood and keep his eyes on the ground'. He wore it for 40 years. His story is thought to have inspired Harry Houdini the famous escapologist.

St Conrad of Piacenza

A fourteenth-century nobleman, Conrad adored hunting and one day had his beaters set light to the undergrowth in order to flush out game. Unfortunately it got out of control and laid waste to half the district. Conrad ran away and a poor peasant nearby was accused of starting the fire and sentenced to death. To save his life Conrad confessed to the crime. He was then presented with a bill to cover the damage the fire had caused and was ruined. He persuaded his wife that this was God's call to a life of self-denial, so he joined the Franciscans and she the Poor Clares. He became terribly famous for holiness and had to hide away in the grotto of Pizzoni. Thousands flocked to him for his prayers were exceptionally powerful. He could make cake appear magically and cure people of their ailments. Wherever he went he was surrounded by fluttering birds. He spent so much time praying in front of a crucifix that he died doing so and it was a couple of days before anyone realised that he was actually dead. His intercession is particularly sought by those suffering from hernias.

St Onesimus

He was a run-away slave who became the amanuensis of St Paul and subject of his shortest epistle. He lived in the household of Philemon, a wealthy Christian of Colossae, but absconded after he was caught with his hand in the till, or so it is said. He ended up with St Paul, who liked him so much – Onesimus means 'helpful' – that he wrote to Philemon asking him if he would allow him to make restitution for the crime. Philemon agreed to this and Onesimus returned home. He eventually became a bishop but came to a sticky end, martyred by being clubbed to death. Some think he is the person who wrote the letters of Paul that are not by Paul, though many disagree. His name, pleasingly, suggests he could be the patron saint of the onesie.

Blessed Peter de Geremia

Born in Palermo in 1381 he was a gifted child and went to the University of Bologna where he excelled at the law. On the brink of a brilliant career he went to bed one night, dreaming of the successes and honours to come, when the ghost of a kinsman, a famous lawyer, appeared outside his third floor window and said the world's pomps and empty show were not really worth the candle and to think on lest he join him in the realms infernal. Peter experienced an immediate conversion and the next day got a blacksmith to forge him a chain which he wore ever after as a penance. He became a Dominican and soon Prior of his abbey, and wrought fearful miracles. Begging for alms one day a fisherman told him to sling his hook and all the fish in his nets jumped out and swam to the saint on the shore. The fishermen said sorry and the fish all jumped back in them again (and the friars had free fish for life).

On another occasion he was preaching when Mount Etna erupted and everyone screamed for fear of the lava pouring towards them. Peter merely took the veil covering the face of a statue of St Agatha and waved it around. The lava reversed back into the volcano and everyone was saved. He is the patron of penitent lawyers; rather a sinecure as patronages go.

St Rose of Lima

Born in 1586 in Peru, she was the daughter of a Puerto Rican harquebusier and a part-Incan mother. When she was a baby her nurse saw her face miraculously transformed into a rose, so at her confirmation she took Rose as her name. She was terribly pious and adored performing severe penances, cutting off her hair, for example, when someone said how pretty she looked, rubbing chilli peppers into her face, and holding her hands over a flame. She also fasted three times a week, received Holy Communion daily, and took a vow of chastity, to her father's chagrin. At first she used to wander round Lima selling her needlework and inviting the destitute back to her room where she'd give them her lunch, but eventually she became a recluse, praying through the night in a little grotto she made herself and having ecstasies. She also flogged herself thrice daily, wore a hair shirt, a spiked crown concealed by roses, and an iron chain about her waist, dragging a heavy cross round and round the garden, which became rather tiresome for her family. She would eat nothing for days, and drink only a draught of gall mixed with bitter herbs. When she could no longer stand up she made a bed of broken glass and thorns and lay down on that. It all became too much for her, and she died aged thirty-one. After her death the Church authorities removed her head from her body so it could be sent on tours of the country to edify the faithful. She is patroness of Peru, florists and arguing families.

St Fridolin

Known as the Irish Wanderer, he was an indefatigable seventh-century missionary who was led by a vision to the body of St Hilary at Poitiers, which he dug up, and thereafter he roamed Europe founding monasteries in his name. He became friendly with one Urso, a Swiss landowner, who left him land when he died, but the legacy was disputed by the family.

To prove his claim, Fridolin raised the decomposing body of Urso to give evidence on his behalf, which the court found persuasive. Eventually Fridolin came to Säckingen, on the Rhine, where he founded a famous monastery on an island that became terribly famous for its school, a sporty place where the boys played games all day long.

St Eutychius of Phrygia

As a young man in Troas he encountered St Paul on one of his missionary journeys. A crowd had gathered to hear the great apostle preach and Eutychius found a place on a window ledge overlooking the scene. Instead of the customary 10 to 12 minutes we are used to today Paul was still

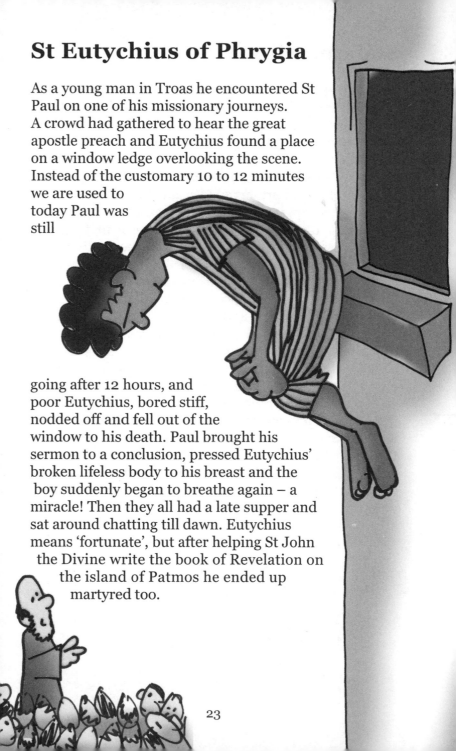

going after 12 hours, and poor Eutychius, bored stiff, nodded off and fell out of the window to his death. Paul brought his sermon to a conclusion, pressed Eutychius' broken lifeless body to his breast and the boy suddenly began to breathe again – a miracle! Then they all had a late supper and sat around chatting till dawn. Eutychius means 'fortunate', but after helping St John the Divine write the book of Revelation on the island of Patmos he ended up martyred too.

St Januarius

He was responsible for a charming miracle which I have witnessed. He was Bishop of Naples in the early fourth century and was martyred by Diocletian who had him thrown to some bears (which were disinclined to eat him), cast into a furnace (from which he emerged unscathed) and finally beheaded. The saint's holy blood was collected and preserved by a lady called Eusebia and today is kept in an ampoule by the city of Naples, the 'urbs sanguinum', of which Januarius is first among its 50 patron saints. Three times a year the cardinal archbishop collects the ampoule from the mayor and carries it in a procession to the monastery of Santa Chiara where the blood, now a brownish dried lump, is put on the high altar and everyone prays like mad. Miraculously, the dried-up lump liquefies, signifying prosperity for Naples in the year ahead. A man waves a hanky as a sign to the army, which greets the news with a 21-gun salute. I have attended one of these ceremonies and a grand day out is had by all. It greatly impressed Nietzsche, who in book four of The Gay Science treats the liquefaction as a leitmotif, signifying the possibility of the revival of deadened life and an encouragement for all to say an enthusiastic 'Yes' to whatever fate comes our way. Nietzsche later went mad after witnessing a man abuse a horse.

St Renatus of Angers

He was born in the late fourth century in France to a sterile woman called Bononia, who received miraculous fertility treatment from Saint Maurilius, her bishop. Unfortunately the child was born prematurely and very feeble, and although Bononia called for the bishop to save him, he was in the middle of a senior staff meeting and could not get away until it was too late. Maurilius was stricken with remorse and stowed away on a boat for England, throwing the keys to the cathedral into the sea where they were swallowed by a passing fish. In England he became a fashionable gardener, replanting the royal borders with remarkable flair, but seven years later the fish arrived back at Angers, coughed up the keys, and told everyone where the bishop was.

Maurilius then had a vision, sleep-walked all the way home, made his way to the child's tomb and nutted it. The child came back to life and St Maurilius baptised him Renatus – reborn. Renatus eventually succeeded Maurilius as bishop but retired to a cave in Sorrento where he wore a sack and did nothing all day. He is one of the phallic saints, good for restoring male potency, because his name was thought to be close to the old French word for kidneys, which were thought then to be the organs responsible for that sort of thing.

St Acca of Hexham

A seventh-century monk of Northumbria whom God blessed with a glorious singing voice. He was a protégé of Bosa of York and then Wilfrid of Ripon, who vouchsafed him a vision of an English church filled with gorgeous singing and bibelots. When he became Abbot of Hexham he head-hunted a famous singer called Maban to train his monks as backing singers in the Gregorian style, then all the rage. Wedded to the spirit of the day unfortunately he was swiftly widowed. Tastes changed and he was exiled to Whithorn.

St Richard Gwyn

A Catholic from Wrexham at the time of the Reformation, he was threatened with ghastliness if he did not conform to the Church of England. Wavering, a miraculous murder of crows appeared and screeched at him for his pusillanimity. He then took to making up comic songs about the vicar for which he was clapped in irons. He then rattled his chains during sermons which so annoyed everyone he was convicted of high treason, though during the trial the lawyers were all struck blind and dumb. He was hanged, drawn and quartered in Wrexham's Beast Market on 17 October in 1584 having apologised for being rude to the vicar.

St Cecilia

'In a garden shady this holy lady
With reverent cadence and subtle psalm,
Like a black swan as death came on
Poured forth her song in perfect calm.'

She was an early Christian martyr who became the patron saint of musicians. Her feast day is celebrated on 22 November.

St Hildebrand of Fossombrone

He was Provost of Rimini and there preached so resolutely against the licentiousness of its people that his flock threatened to kill him and he had to run away. In 1170 he was consecrated bishop of Fossombrone and lived to be a hundred and one. On his death bed his cook thought he needed a good dinner so brought him a dish of roast partridges, even though it was Lent and the meat of fowls forbidden. The old bishop raised his hand over his lunch and the partridges turned into tortoises and crept very slowly away. A relic of him was sold recently on eBay for $395.

St Zosimas

A monk of the fifth century, who at a very young age joined a monastery in Palestine and became known for his wisdom and asceticism. The best-known story about Zosimas connects him to another saintly and extraordinary figure of the age. Zosimas was wandering around the desert one Lent reflecting on his sins, when he ran into Mary of Egypt, the hairiest woman in antiquity. She asked if he'd kindly lend her his cloak and he obliged. In return she demonstrated her psychic gifts. Then she asked him if he would return the following year and bring her Holy Communion on Jordan's bank. He did and she walked on the water to receive it. Come back next year, she asked, and he did but found her dead, though miraculously incorrupt. He buried her body with the assistance of a passing lion and went home. Zosimas himself lived to be almost a hundred years old.

St Paul the Hermit

Caught up in the persecution of Decius in 250, he was
betrayed to the Roman soldiers by his brother-in-law,
who would have inherited his property in the event of his
death. Paul fled to the desert and there lived under a palm
tree next to a spring, dressed in palm leaves and surviving
on dates and water, until he was forty-three, when a
raven started to come every day with a morsel of bread
in its beak. When Paul turned a hundred years old word
reached him of Antony of Egypt, the most celebrated
desert hermit, and the two both claimed have served God
longest in the austerities of their eremitical lives. I'm
afraid it all got a bit competitive. In the end Antony was
led to Paul by a she-wolf, and when the raven arrived with
two morsels of bread, Paul invited Antony for luncheon.
Paul invited the ninety-year-old abbot to break the bread,
but Antony deferred to his elder, and it would have
staled and remained uneaten had it not miraculously
broken itself. Paul then told Antony he fancied he would
die and would he please wrap his body in the cloak of
St Athanasius. Antony rushed
home to fetch it and by the time
he returned he found Paul dead.
He exchanged Paul's palm-leaf
garment for the saint's robe and
two lions came along and dug
his grave. Thereafter, Antony
wore the palm leaf garment
at Easter and Pentecost
in affectionate
remembrance of
his host.

St Vitalis of Gaza

He was one of the first Savers of Fallen Women. He was a monk in seventh-century Gaza, but at the age of sixty left the monastery behind and travelled to Alexandria, where he diligently obtained the name and address of every prostitute in the city. He then hired himself out as a labourer and at the end of each day gave his wages to one of the prostitutes so she could have a day off, telling them that their dignity as women was sacred and should not be debased by selling themselves to satisfy the lust of men. Many abandoned their profession as a result, which went down badly with their clients, one of whom hit him over the head in a brothel. Vitalis staggered home and died. At his funeral all the city's prostitutes came out to follow the coffin, carrying candles. He started rather a vogue, and among those who followed him into this ministry was The Revd Harold Davidson, Rector of Stiffkey in Norfolk in the 1920s, who unfortunately ended up being eaten by a lion in Skegness.

Toyohiko Kagawa

Toyohiko Kagawa was born in Kobe, Japan in 1888 to a sex-addicted businessman and a concubine. Sent away to school he was taken in by two American missionaries and converted to Christianity, which provoked his parents to disown him. After studying theology, embryology, genetics, comparative anatomy and paleontology at Princeton he became convinced that Christianity in action was the only kind of Christianity he was interested in, so returned to Kobe to live and work in its slums, where he liked to go around holding hands with murderers. This produced a major work, his 'Researches in the Psychology of the Poor', which did for Japanese society in the 1920s what Mayhew's 'London Labour and the London Poor' did for British society in the 1850s. His argument was that the Church, uniting with the cooperative movement and the peace movement, could provide the only workable alternative to capitalism, state socialism, and fascism. This, however, was unattractive to the authorities and he was thrown into prison, so he invented three-dimensional forestry instead, and persuaded farmers to plant walnut trees to protect against soil erosion and to provide nuts to nourish their pigs. He argued tirelessly against Japanese militarism and imperialism, was nominated for Nobel Prizes for both peace and literature, and after his death in 1960 was declared a Sacred Treasure, an honour shared with Peter Parker, not Spider-Man, but the former chairman of British Rail. 'I read in a book that a man called Christ went about doing good,' he said. 'It is very disconcerting to me that I am so easily satisfied with just going about.' That was Kagawa, not Sir Peter.

St Mel

St Mel accidentally consecrated the first woman bishop.
He was a nephew of St Patrick in the sixth century and
accompanied him on his missionary travels to Ireland.
In spite of some gossip about an improper relationship
with his Auntie Lipait, Mel was consecrated bishop of
Armagh – or perhaps Ardagh, it is not clear – by his
Uncle Patrick. As bishop, Mel presided over St Bridget's
solemn profession as a nun but unfortunately he lost
his place in the book and before anyone realised what
was happening consecrated her as a bishop. The clergy
protested, but St Mel believed it was the will of God and
upheld the consecration as valid. I've no idea how they
sorted this out, if they ever did. He is the patron saint of
bishops who seek to ordain women to the episcopate.

St Jerome

One of the four Latin Doctors of the Church and the patron saint of translators. A brilliant student in fifth-century Rome, whose bouts of hedonism were curbed by visits to the catacombs where, among the rotting dead, he resolved to follow a life of asceticism. He became a Christian and devoted himself to the study of theology and Scripture. To fund his unworldliness he preyed on rich widows, with whom he was often accused of having affairs, and it is known that he killed one by insisting she follow an impossibly ascetic regime. Under a cloud, he left Rome for the desert, where he translated the Bible into Latin (the Vulgate) – one of the greatest and most influential achievements in scholarship. He also made friends with a lion, who came to him with a thorn in its paw, and an owl. He ended up living in a shed near Bethlehem, but this got smashed up when he upset the Pelagians. He is often seen in paintings with a smart red cardinal's hat to which he was not entitled.

St Cannera of Inis Cathaig

She was a sixth-century anchoress from Bantry and lived very quietly walled up in her cell until she realised she was dying and thought it expedient to seek the Last Rites. Inspired by a vision of a shaft of golden light she went to the island monastery of Senan, miraculously walking across the water to get there. Unfortunately the monks there were all scared of ladies and the abbot said he was terribly sorry but as a daughter of Eve she was a contaminant and couldn't come in. Cannera told them not to be so silly adding, 'Christ came to redeem women no less than to redeem men' and that if He sought the company of women then they should too. In the end they grudgingly allowed her to receive the sacrament and when she died they buried her at the island's edge and in due course sought to re-assert there the idea of male supremacy. It is perhaps too obvious to offer this as a model for the Church's attitude to women even today, but I do so nonetheless. Interestingly, another exclusive male society, that of sailors, is more warmly disposed to Cannera. They take pebbles from the island as a protection against shipwreck.

St Balthild of Ascania

She was born in East Anglia in the seventh century of royal blood, but unfortunately was sold into slavery and ended up a kitchen maid in the household of Erchinoald, an official of the Frankish King Clovis II. She was exceptionally comely, neat and tidy, and loved to sing while cleaning the lavatory. When Erchinoald's wife died he took to chasing her round the kitchens and she had to hide. However, she caught the king's eye and he fell in love with her. They married. Balthild became Queen of the Franks, and in due course the mother of three kings, Clotaire, Childeric and Theuderic. She remained, however, modest and humble, never forgetting her years of captivity and was one of the earliest advocates for the abolition of the slave trade. This is on the plus side. On the minus side she was rather a notorious killer, responsible for the murder of at least nine bishops, according to one source.

Anyway, she eventually forsook her royal rank and lived out her days in a convent. When she died the Virgin Mary kindly let down a ladder from heaven and up she went.

St Albert the Great

He was born in the thirteenth century to a noble family and adored hunting, but then came under the influence of Jordan, The Siren of the Schools, who admitted him to the Dominican order. Surrounded by brilliant students there he realised he was not as clever as he thought he was and tried to escape by climbing over the wall but the Virgin Mary pushed him off a ladder and bestowed on him the Gift of Science. He became the greatest mind of his generation until St Thomas Aquinas, his student, surpassed him. Unfortunately the pope made him a bishop, which he loathed. He eschewed all episcopal finery and chose instead a rough pair of boots which earned him the nickname St Clodhopper. His clergy loathed him and he went back to teaching. He was a brilliant scholar, writing extensively in the fields of botany, astronomy, chemistry, physics, biology, metaphysics, ethics, scripture, geography, geology (he once demonstrated the earth is spherical), logic, mathematics, theology, and meteorology. He made a mechanical head out of brass which could answer any question put to it and gave his name to the typeface Albertus. He is patron saint of Those Who Find the Tension between Faith and Science Creative Rather than Frightening.

St John the Golden-Mouthed

A fourth-century Archbishop of Constantinople, preacher and controversialist, and one of the most important Fathers of the Early Church. He seems to have had awkward relationships with women, particularly the vain and dressy Empress Aelia Eudoxia, who banished him twice for criticising her dress sense. While living as a hermit in the desert he mistook a princess in distress for a demon, and refused her aid. She managed to persuade him that she was a good Christian girl and vulnerable to wild beasts so he reluctantly let her into his cave, first carefully partitioning it along gender lines. Unfortunately they surrendered to the sin of fornication, and John, stricken with guilt, pushed her off a cliff, which was hardly gallant. Remorseful, he vowed he would live as a beast of the field until his sins were expiated and for years lived on all fours eating grass. Fortunately the princess appeared alive, suckling his baby, which miraculously pronounced his sins forgiven.

St Cunigunde of Luxembourg

Around the end of the tenth century she contracted a
'white marriage' with the Holy Roman Emperor Henry
II. He was a great sweetie, but gave all their money
away and died leaving her a poor widow. She entered
a convent where she wrought rather modest miracles,
putting out small fires by making the sign of the
cross and slapping frivolous novices leaving on their
blushing faces mysterious, unfading welts.

St Justus of Beauvais

The youngest cephalophore in the calendar. He was born in the third century to a Christian in what we now call Auxerre. When he was nine his uncle was arrested for being a Christian so he went with his father to ransom him from the Roman authorities. Unfortunately on the way he was accused of being a magician by some soldiers and beheaded. Imagine their surprise when he immediately picked up his own head and started preaching a sermon so persuasive many were converted to the faith. There was, of course, a roaring trade in his relics. A monk of Malmedy in Belgium claimed to have obtained his body 'for a good price', but this does not tally with the claim of Winchester Cathedral to have a fair chunk of his head in its treasury, donated by King Athelstan. Chur in Switzerland and Zutphen in the Netherlands claim to have parts of him too.

St Emmeram of Regensburg

He was a seventh-century bishop who suffered an unusually protracted martyrdom. He held office between the death of Dido and the ascension of Ansoaldus, but it went wrong when the Duke's unwedded daughter Uta became pregnant. To mitigate her shame Emmeram said he was the father – he wasn't – so the Duke had him bound to a ladder and cut him to pieces, bit by bit, starting with his fingertips. As his suffering reached its climax he asked for water and his friend who was keeping him company replied, 'Why do you seek relief, when nothing of you remains but your stubby trunk, undecorated with limbs?'. Emmeram, understandably discouraged, died and as proof of his innocence, a magic ladder was lowered to bear him to heaven.

St Denis

St Denis is perhaps the most celebrated of the cephalophores. He was Bishop of Paris in the third century but very greatly irked the pagan priests by poaching their devotees. Eventually he was taken to the the Martyrs' Mountain (Montmartre) and there beheaded. After his head was chopped off he picked it up and walked six miles preaching an encouraging sermon. This has posed problems for artists, who were not quite sure where the halo should go on a saint carrying his own head (cephalophore). Some put it on the severed head, some over the stump of his neck, others had St Denis carry it in his other hand. Also there was a dispute over how much of the head he carried, for churches in Paris squabbled over who got what of his relics, some claiming they had the crown which was chopped off by the executioner's first ill-aimed blow. For these reasons he is patron saint of those with headaches (as well as the frenzied and hydrophobes).

St Arcadius of Mauretania

He was caught up in the persecutions of Christians in the early fourth century. Arcadius was obliged to offer sacrifices to idols, but refused. This so annoyed the judge that instead of beheading him straight away he had Arcadius' limbs hacked off, one by one. You might think this would put one out, but Arcadius addressed his butchered parts, saying, 'Ooh, now you are happy, hacked off arms and legs, for now you belong to God,' and died.

St Adrian of Nicomedia

He was a third-century Roman soldier and a guard
of the Emperor Galerius Maximian. One day he was
torturing some Christians but they seemed so nice he
decided to become a Christian too, which meant he was
immediately thrown into his own jail and was horribly
tortured. His wife, Natalie, came to see him dressed
up as a boy and asked if he would kindly put in a good
word for her when he got to heaven and he was then
hacked to pieces. The body parts were thrown on a fire
but a miraculous storm put it out and Natalie managed
to grab a hand, which she
took home for a souvenir.
Adrian is 'patron saint of
communications phenomena'.
A relic of St Adrian was
recently sold on eBay for
$125 + p&p.

St Lambert

He was Bishop of Maastricht from 670 to 700, when he was murdered. He was pierced through the heart by a javelin while at the altar. His predecessor, Theodard, was also murdered, but not long after this Lambert's patron Childeric II was also murdered and the majordomo of Neustria expelled him from his see and he spent seven years in exile. Lambert's faction then murdered Dodo the Domesticus of Pepin, so Dodo's people had Lambert murdered too, an unfortunate occurrence, but his supporters successfully construed this as a martyrdom arguing Lambert died defending marital fidelity when he denounced the king Pepin, married to Plectrude, for dallying with Dodo's daughter. All's well that ends well, and today Lambert is remembered with the Lambertusfest, a two week celebration culminating on the eve of his feast when children heap branches into 'Lambert pyramids' which they decorate with lanterns and then dance round them singing traditional songs known as Lambertussingen.

St John the Gold Gusher

An eighth-century Arab Christian from Damascus who followed his father into the administration of the Muslim caliphate. John, a brilliant scholar, eventually became chief administrator before entering a monastery. He was good at everything, excelling at music, astronomy and Pythagoras and Euclid in adding up and taking away. His cordial relations with the Caliph were somewhat soured when Leo III sent forged documents to him implicating John in a treasonable plot. The Caliph, miffed, had John's hand cut off and displayed for all to see. After a couple of days of this, John prayed to an icon of Mary, then asked for his hand back and miraculously reattached it to his arm. As a thank you John attached a silver hand to the icon, which thereafter became known as the 'three-hander'.

St Rhipsime

She was an Armenian virgin who lived in a convent in
Rome. She was exceptionally comely, so comely she
attracted the attention of the Emperor Diocletian and
had to flee with her Sisters to Vagharshapat, ruled
by the wicked King Tiridates III. Diocletian heard of
this and insisted the King send Rhipsime back to him
in Rome, but she said she was unable to oblige being
betrothed to Jesus Christ. Tiridates lost his temper
and had Rhipsime tortured; her tongue was cut out,
she was blinded, disembowelled, and her body cut into
pieces, and then all her Sisters were thrown to the lions.
Feeling smug and pleased with themselves, the king
and his soldiers were suddenly beset by vengeful devils
who turned them into wild animals and sent them
running through the forest, gnawing at their limbs.
Wicked King Tiridates was turned into a wild boar but
was saved by St Gregory the Illuminator who happened
to be passing by. A shrine was built to Rhipsime when
Jesus descended from heaven in a shaft of light and
smote a certain spot with a golden hammer creating
a tiny earthquake. She gave her name to Rhipsime
Kurshudyan, the Armenian lady weightlifter and 2012
Olympic bronze medallist.

St Catalina of Palma

She was an orphan in Majorca in the sixteenth century and grew up in the household of her wicked uncle who was beastly to her. In the end she ran away and became a domestic servant in the convent of Saint Mary Magdalen in Palma. Before long, signs of her sanctity began to appear. She fell into trances and floated up to the ceiling where she revolved, uttering prophecies and sprouting stigmata, which were tended by angels and saints. She fell into ecstasies so readily and so often that she would quite often wash up and sweep the floors while in one. She was known also to break off from tidying to wrestle with the forces of darkness. There's a lovely fiesta in her honour in Valdemossa when the children dress up and sit on her Triumphal Car which goes round and round the town.

St Benedict Labre

One of the strangest and greatest saints in the calendar. He was born in northern France in 1748 the son of a prosperous shopkeeper. He was already prodigiously holy while in the womb, according to his mother, which gave her the collywobbles. He was educated by his uncle, a priest, but was terribly bullied by one of his servants. The young Benedict accepted this treatment without complaint and began to adopt the austerities that were to be the signal characteristic of his life, replacing his pillow with a plank of wood, and taking on endless chores. After his uncle died he tried to join the great and austere monastery of La Trappe but he was too austere even for them so in the end he took to the streets and became a beggar. After wandering round Europe for some years, dressed in an old sack eating the beads of his rosary, he ended up in Rome and there lived the life of a tramp, wandering from church to church where he would contemplate the sacred mysteries with such intense devotion he became known as the 'beggar of the perpetual adoration'. His fame spread and Cavallucci painted a wonderful portrait of him. Around this time he started levitating. He was so familiar a sight hovering in the great Basilicas that sacristans used to wait for him to get airborne and sweep under him instead of round him. Eventually, weakened by his austerities, he collapsed on the steps of his favourite church, Santa Maria dei Monti, during Holy Week and was taken to a butcher's shop where he died. He is the patron saint of the victims of ill-thought-through, unjust, short-sighted and downright cruel housing policy.

St Ambrose

He was born in the fourth century and as a baby a swarm of bees settled on his face and left a drop of honey on his lips as a sign of his extraordinary gifts as a preacher. He was forced by a shouting child to become Bishop of Milan in spite of torturing people and inviting prostitutes round to recuse himself from this post. The people would have none of it and he was baptised, ordained and consecrated bishop in a week. Once enthroned he gave all his wealth away and put down various things fiercely. He was extraordinarily learned, the first person to read without speaking the words aloud, according to his famous convert St Augustine of Hippo. He is credited with inventing antiphonal chant, the call and response kind, and also a liturgy which is rather Book of Common Prayer – the peace comes before the offertory and there's quite a lot of penitence for the faithful to express. It is still in use today. He is patron of beekeepers, geese, and the French army's logistical corps.

St Theodore of Sykeon

He was born in the seventh century, the bastard child of a strumpet and a man who had a circus act doing acrobatics on a camel. He grew up in the strumpet's bawdy house, which she kept with her sister, but when he was six she had him baptised, dressed in a fine tunic and sent off to the imperial court. Then St George appeared to her in a dream and said this was not the way forward so he came home and went to school instead. Around this time the strumpets employed an old man as a chef at their bawdy house who turned out to be a culinary genius. His imaginative use of locally sourced ingredients combined with a brilliant palate and fabulous creativity soon turned it into place of pilgrimage for foodies. Interestingly around this time, after a scrape with bubonic plague, Theodore began to eschew good cooking and adopted the ascetic habits of a holy man, overnighting in a cave and eating only raw vegetables. Then he joined a monastery, was ordained priest and started wearing an iron girdle and breastplate and chains around his arms and legs. In the end, at his request, he was locked into an iron cage which hung from a chain suspended in mid-air above the entrance to his cave. He became a great seer and prophet and once dashed an ornate chalice from the hand of a bishop for he divined that it had been made from a strumpet's chamber pot. Aged one hundred, and against his wishes, he was made a bishop. He went around looking frightful, with untrimmed hair and nails and eyebrows which wound their way round his whole head. He was so annoying a prominent layman pushed him off a chair He retired, coming out only to cure the emperor's son of elephantiasis.

St Jean de Brébeuf

A Jesuit missionary to Canada who was martyred by the Iroquois in 1649. A Frenchman, he lived with the native Huron people learning their customs and language and wrote the first dictionary of their tongue ('Jesuit', by the way, is 'hatitsihenstaatsi', 'they are charcoal'). He was a gentle giant, extremely strong, and made himself helpful around the place. But progress was extremely slow, though he did write them a nice carol, and he had to go back to Quebec for a while because the Huron kept blaming him for crop failures and the outbreak of plague. Unfortunately the Huron went to war with the Iroquois, who captured and martyred Brébeuf and his companions cruelly, tying them to stakes, mock-baptising them with boiling water, giving them necklaces of red hot iron hatchet-heads, scalping them and mutilating them. Brébeuf endured his suffering with such patience they cut his heart out and ate it to acquire his courage. It is said he gave lacrosse its name for he thought its participants looked like lady bishops.

St Demetrius

He is known as the Myrrh-Streamer. He was born into a noble family in Thessalonica in the third century, but got into trouble for being a Christian and was arrested and confined to a bath house by Maximian. The Games came to town and a boastful wrestler named Lyaeus was so annoying that Demetrius' friend Nestor came to him and asked him for a miraculous intervention to defeat Lyaeus. This was forthcoming and when Nestor smote him the former boaster fell lifeless to the ground. Maximian, who had money on Lyaeus, was so cross, he had Nestor slain with his own sword and Demetrius run through with lances while he was relaxing by a swimming pool. Demetrius' servant Lupus retrieved his blood stained signet ring and used this to effect so many miracles Maximian had him beheaded too. Nestor and Demetrius were buried together in the swimming pool where he had met his fate, but ever after it ran with sweet-smelling myrrh so abundantly the sides were all but worn away.

St Hilarion

Anchorite and camel tamer, born to pagan parents in
Gaza at the end of the third century, He was a tremendous
socialite and adored going to the theatre and watching
gladiators until he converted to Christianity in Alexandria.
Thereafter he became a disciple of St Anthony Abbot
and one of the most famous ascetics of his day. He found
Anthony's monastery a bit crowded so he set off into the
desert with only a shirt, a cloak and a blanket and lived
on dried figs which he ate at night. He was unfortunately
beset by carnal thoughts which he warded off by weaving
baskets and restricting his diet to a few roots. He lived in
a tiny hut built of reeds where he sang hymns and heard
cats and dogs talking. It was here he one day miraculously
tamed a mad Bactrian camel. He never changed nor
washed his clothes and was once beset by robbers, but
they left him alone and mended their ways because his
smell upset them. He perhaps unwisely used his powers
to get a chap called Italicus to win a chariot race and
was pestered thereafter for the rest of his life and had to
move around a lot. Eventually he fled to the mountains of
Cyprus, where he died in 371.

St Leger

He was a seventh-century Bishop of Autun who fell out spectacularly with the Bishops of Chalons and Valence, who addressed their issues with their brother bishop by boring out his eyes with a gimlet, cauterising the sockets, pulling out his tongue and cutting his lips off. Eventually he was murdered too. St Leger is today remembered by lending his name, indirectly, to the oldest classic horse race in England.

St Edith of Wilton

She was born at the end of the tenth century, the illegitimate daughter of Edgar the Peaceful, who abducted her mother. She became a nun, renowned for her learning, beauty and her fondness for wearing luxurious garments woven from spun gold. When Ethelwold of Winchester rebuked her for this she said, 'a mind may be as pure under these vestments as under your tattered furs'. After she died she beat up the devil and then told St Dunstan that if he exhumed her body it would give off a nice smell, which it did.

St Paul the Simple

He was a farmer in fourth-century Egypt, but when he was sixty he came home from the fields to find his wife canoodling with one of the neighbours. 'Oh well,' he said to the man, 'You take her. I'm off to be a hermit.' He went to see St Anthony Abbot in the desert and asked if he would mind if he became his disciple. St Anthony refused because of his age, but instead of going away Paul just sat outside with nothing to eat or drink. After four days and nights St Anthony took him in for fear that he would die. At supper St Anthony took a single morsel of bread, as was his habit, and gave three to Paul, but Paul only ate one. 'Won't you have some more?' asked St Anthony, but Paul said, 'If one crust is sufficient for you, then one is sufficient for me, but thanks very much for asking'. Impressed by his simplicity and lovely manners St Anthony took him in; a wise decision, for Paul turned out to be a dear and wrought miracles. He was also very good at casting out demons by arguing Scripture with them and in really difficult cases beating the person possessed with a sheepskin. Eventually the demons turned into dragons and scuttled off.

St Amador of Portugal

He was a hermit of São Pedro Vir-on-Corces, where he lived for many years rather pestered by a notorious lady called Ricarda, who had form for stalking and anti-social behavoiur. Desperate for a quiet life it appears that Amador fathered her son, although this is disputed. She certainly turned up one day with a boy whom she claimed was his, and Amador asked to baptise him. Ricarda refused which made the little boy burst into tears because he was frightened that, unbaptised, he would be prey to demons.

He was; at that very moment the ground opened up and some particularly nasty demons appeared and dragged the boy and Ricarda to the edge of the pit. Down they went and Ricarda was never seen again. Amador prayed for the boy, however, and he landed 'without receiving any harm to his feet' and was restored to his father. A deer came by every day and suckled the child, and eventually he became a priest and a hermit too. In Portugal today St Amador is very often invoked against aphids.

St Andrew the Scot

He was, confusingly, an Irishman, born in the ninth
century and the brother of St Brigid the Younger.
Even more confusingly he is also known as Andrew of
Tuscany and Andrew of Fiesole. As we might infer from
this, he was a restless soul and fell in with St Donatus,
who was elected bishop of Fiesole thanks to the
intervention of a miraculous voice. Pleased as punch,
Donatus declared Andrew his archdeacon. He was a
great thaumaturge and was especially good at healing
sick girls, casting out demons, restoring sight to the
blind, and miraculously restoring derelict churches . He
served Donatus for 50 years, an exhausting enterprise,
which eventually killed him.

As he lay on his deathbed an angel visited his sister
Brigid in Ireland as she sat eating a supper of fish and
salad. He picked her up and flew her to Fiesole so she
could help out with her brother's intimate care. He was
so pleased to see her he stood up on his hard pallet and
waved his arms about. Then he was bathed in a brilliant
light, gave forth the odour of roses, and dropped
down dead. He was buried in one of the churches he
miraculously restored but they forgot where and one
day a dead floozie was shoved in on top of him. He
complained in a vision, but the vicar did nothing about
it, so he afflicted him with epilepsy until the floozie, by
now putrefied, was removed.

Blessed Margaret of Metola

She was a poor little blind girl who so disappointed her parents they abandoned her in a church. Raised on the parish, she was passed from family to family, and quickly acquired a reputation for holiness. She could turn naughty children good and liked especially to chastise the spiritually idle, who were delighted when she chose to enter a convent.

There, despite her blindness, she received startling visions, got into terrible fights with demons, and sent her magic cloak round the town to put out fires. On her death bed she exclaimed, 'If only you knew what was in my heart!' When she finally expired they opened her up and found in her heart three perfect pearls into which scenes from the life of Jesus had been miraculously carved.

St Donagh of Fiesole

Rather than being born great or achieving greatness, he had greatness thrust upon him. He was born in Ireland in the ninth century and became a poet, wandering round composing odes. He went on holiday to Rome with a handsome young friend called Andrew to look at the tombs of the apostles, but on the way home they called in at Fiesole. The city was at that time beset by demons and everyone was gathered in the cathedral to pray for deliverance from them. At that very moment Donagh stepped over the threshold, and all the candles miraculously lit themselves and all the bells pealed of their own accord. Naturally, everyone recognised that Donagh was the answer to their prayers, so they made him their bishop although he didn't really know what was going on. They made his friend Andrew his deacon, though he didn't understand what was happening either. Fortunately it worked out rather well. They all got on famously; Donagh gave poetry-writing lessons and kept everyone amused with his odes of old Ireland. Here's an example, translated from the Latin:

'No savage bear with lawless fury roves,
Nor fiercer lion through her peaceful
    groves;
No poison there infects,
No scaly snake creeps through the grass,
Nor frog annoys the lake.'

He also wrote his own, rather boastful, epitaph.

St Saturnine

He was present at the Last Supper, although not in the VIP area, and later consecrated by St Peter as the first Bishop of Toulouse. There he annoyed the pagan priests because whenever he was around their oracles would remain silent. One day they grabbed him and ordered him to sacrifice to idols but he refused, so they tied him by the ankles to a bull and had him dragged around the town until 'his head was all broken and his brain sprang out'. Finally, at a place called Matabiau the rope broke. The Matabiau was traditionally the place where the bull copped it in the bloody rites of Mithras, which climaxed with the tauroctony (bull killing). Thus we can see how the early Christians took over existing religious practices and adapted them – or indeed subverted them – so that they witnessed to the verities of the Gospel. For a brilliant exploration of how this works I strongly commend the writings of professor René Girard.

St Vincent of Saragossa

He was a deacon at the turn of the fourth century in Spain, and one of his jobs was to look after his bishop Valerius, who had a stammer. The governor of the region, Dacian, unleashed a terrible persecution and Valerius was brought before him, but because of the bishop's speech impediment Vincent did the talking. Dacian grew so impatient that he released Valerius and submitted Vincent to hideous tortures in the bishop's place. He was racked, torn with iron hooks, and roasted on a grid iron. He survived all this without uttering a word, or surrendering the holy Scriptures to be be cast into a furnace, so Dacian had his servant smash a whole load of crockery on the floor of the dungeon and then threw Vincent into it to add to his agonies. A mysterious light and the odour of flowers flooded the cell, so impressively that the jailer immediately converted to Christianity. People kept coming to kiss his sores and dip cloths in his blood so his death was hastened and his body thrown into a wilderness to be eaten by wild animals.

A raven came and guarded him, however and the wild animals left him alone. So Dacian had the saint's body tied to a millstone and thrown into the sea but it kept getting washed back up on the shore. His body was eventually recovered and a church built to house his relics which continued to be guarded by ravens. His relics were eventually translated to Lisbon, where he is the city's tremendously popular patron. He is also the patron of sailors, schoolgirls, the vinegar trade, roofers and is very good for protecting fields from frost.

Blessed Noel Pinot

He is patron saint of the properly dressed.
He was a parish priest in eighteenth-century
France and refused to take the oath of loyalty
to the Revolution when it swept to power.
For this he was deprived of his parish but
carried on his ministry clandestinely. One
day he was captured by soldiers while
saying Mass, given a rather perfunctory
trial and sentenced to death. He ascended
the scaffold correctly vested for Mass,
arguing that being guillotined was no
reason not to tie your amice properly
and find a maniple in
the correct liturgical
colour.

St Padarn

He was a British monk of the sixth century who went
to Jerusalem with St David and St Teilo and gained the
gift of tongues, consecration as a bishop, and a nice
top, which came to be venerated as one of the Thirteen
Treasures of the Island of Britain. It was so nice that
when they got home King Arthur came round and
asked that the saint make him a present of it. Padarn
refused and Arthur went off in a huff returning with
some soldiers to demand he hand it over, ululating in
an unfriendly way, and stamping so hard he flattened
the uneven ground he stood upon. Padarn replied, 'May
the earth swallow him,' and immediately the ground
opened up and swallowed the king up to his chin, which
shut him up.

Eventually he begged Padarn's forgiveness and was
released, never to bother him about the top or anything
else again. The other Twelve Treasures of the Island of
Britain are the sword of Rhydderch Hael; the hamper of
Gwyddno Garanhir; the horn of Brân Galed; the chariot
of Morgan Mwynfawr; the halter of Clydno Eiddyn;
the knife of Llawfrodedd the Horseman; the cauldron
of Dyrnwch the Giant; the Whetstone of Tudwal
Tudglyd; the crock and dish of Rhygenydd Ysgolhaig;
the chessboard of Gwenddoleu ap Ceidio; the mantle of
Arthur in Cornwall; the mantle of Tegau Gold-Breast;
and the stone and ring of Eluned the Fortunate. They
ended up in the care of Merlin. The name Merlin, by the
way, is derived from a word meaning 'shitty'.

St Patricius, Acatius,

Patricius, Acatius, Menander and Polyenus were
Christians in a town called Prusa in the Roman province
of Bithynia. Prusa had one of the most famous spas
of the empire and the rich and powerful came in their
droves to be pampered and undergo special treatments.
The Proconsul Julius had such a nice time in its hot
springs that he obliged everyone to make sacrifices to
the god Aesculapius and his daughter Hygieia, because
they're worth it.

Menander and Polyenus

Patricius, however, said the healing properties of its cataracts were the work of Jesus, not these false gods, and they had a huge row about arthritis and hives. In the end Julius got so fed up with Patricius he had him thrown into a boiling pool but Julius was unscalded by its waters so he had him and his friends beheaded for being unsporting.

St Martinian

He was born Caesarea of Palestine in the fourth century and at the age of eighteen went to live as a hermit at the 'place of the Ark'. His austerities and wonder-working became known to Zoe, one of the city's leading harlots. Fond of a challenge, she resolved to seduce him and went to his hermitage by night disguised as an old woman seeking shelter. Once admitted she cast off her cloak and did a dance routine for him in her tassels and feathers while offering a bold exegesis of passages from the Old Testament which she felt might encourage Martinian to succumb to her wiles. It appears he was indeed tempted, but pulling himself together, he stuck his feet in the fire as a distraction which made him scream so loudly Zoe gave up and became a hermit herself, lying on the floor and eating only bread and water.

St Macaille of Croghan

He was an Irish prince who went to the bad and became a Chief of Brigands, but was converted by St Patrick and became then a follower of St Mel, who performed the unusual miracle of growing fish from soil to testify to his purity. Unfortunately they had a terrific fall-out. St Mel was consecrating a bishop one day but accidentally skipped a page from the order of service.

St Macaille said the consecration was therefore not valid, but St Mel cited the ecclesiastical get-out clause of ecclesia supplet, which states that the Church mystically corrects the mistakes of its ministers, and would he please go away as he had things to do. Macaille went off in an almighty sulk and only stopped when he was made a bishop too.

St Marcius the Hermit

He lived in a cave near the great monastery of Monte Cassino in the seventh century. The cave was threatened by a huge overhanging rock that became unstable so the monks responsible for health and safety said they would have to loosen it to bring it down in a controlled way. Marcius refused to move out while they did this, but when it finally fell fortunately it missed him. He then took to chaining himself to the ground until St Benedict told him not to be so silly. However, an angel came from time to time bringing him Holy Communion on a spoon.

St Isabelle of France

She is patroness of precocious children. She was a
thirteenth-century princess, the daughter of Louis VIII
and his queen, Blanche of Castile. Queen Blanche was a
great advocate of education for girls and taught Isabelle
Latin, for which she had an extraordinary aptitude.
She became rather a stickler and was very fond of
interrupting the clergy of the cathedral during services
to correct their use of the subjunctive, or making them
recite first declension nouns. Her parents and the Pope
found her rather awkward to marry off, and she refused
the hands of Hugh XI of Lusignan and Conrad IV of
Germany, both of whom were considered a catch. In
the end she retired to a monastery, but could not get
on with their rule of life so rewrote it to suit herself and
made the pope give it his sanction. Even so, she did
not become a nun herself, preferring to live in her own
house nearby.

St Flavian of Constantinople

He succeeded Proclus as Patriarch in 447, but fell foul
of the wicked Chrysaphius, chancellor of Emperor
Theodosius III, by refusing to pay the expected bribe
on his accession. He then denounced Chrysaphius'
godfather, Eutyches the abbot, as a heretic for getting
his Christology wrong. Theodosius convened a council
at Ephesus in 449, known as the Robber Synod.
Everyone was horribly bullied, a letter in support
of Flavian from Pope Leo was not read out, and the
bishops were forced by the imperial guard to sign a
decree declaring Eutyches orthodox, after which the
guard beat Flavian to death. It turned out all right in the
end. When Theodosius died his successor, Marcian, had
Chrysaphius executed and a new, improved Christology
was restored. St Flavian is the Patron Saint of those who
fall victim to synodical chicanery, and has been much in
demand for intercession recently.

Bishops Latimer and Ridley

They were two English bishops put to death on 16
October 1555, in the reign of the Catholic Queen Mary.
They were burned at the stake where the Martyrs'
Memorial now stands in Broad Street in Oxford.
Archbishop Cranmer, shortly to suffer the same fate,
was made to watch their execution. Poor Bishop Ridley
suffered a great deal, because his brother-in-law, to
speed his death, loaded more wood on the pyre, which
dampened rather than accelerated the blaze. Latimer,
according to John Foxe, said to him, 'Be of good
comfort, and play the man, Master
Ridley; we shall this day light
such a candle, by God's grace, in
England, as I trust shall never
be put out.' English people
continued killing each other
in the name of Christ for some
considerable time.

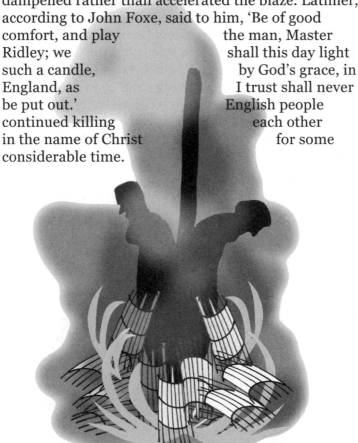

75

St Matilda of Saxony

She lived in the tenth century and grew up in a convent in the care of her Aunt Maud, praying earnestly, and doing lovely needlework. Well suited to the cloistered life, nevertheless her parents married her off to Henry the Fowler, who succeeded Conrad I as King of Germany. He was rather loved by his people and so was Matilda, for as Queen she gave alms liberally and consorted with the poor and the sick, eschewing the gauds and pomps and gewgaws of her high estate. Indeed, when Henry died she cut the jewels from her robes and made little presents of them to favourite clergy. She bore Henry three sons, Otto the Great, Henry the Quarrelsome and St Bruno, but Otto and Henry fell out over the succession and then they turned on her for giving away all her money to the poor and she had to lie low for while. Eventually they were reconciled and she died very contentedly, in sackcloth and ashes, in the year 968.

St Nonnosus

A sixth-century monk who adored cabbages and wished to grow them in a spot where a huge rock lay which even a team of 50 oxen couldn't shift. The saint miraculously tossed it aside as if it were made of polystyrene. He was also good at miraculously producing quantities of oil when the olive harvest failed and restoring smashed glassware. It is also recorded that he had a soothing effect on his bad tempered and despotic abbot. In the eleventh century his relics were taken to Freising in Bavaria but very soon everyone forgot whose relics they were until a wall fell down in 1708 and they were dug up again and re-identified. They were then discovered to be very efficacious in healing diseases of the kidney, and those so afflicted were encouraged to crawl round his sarcophagus four times while moaning in a ritual called the Durchschlüpfsbrauch. It will be a comfort to many that he is also patron of students and scholars experiencing education-related anguish.

St Eloi

He is patron saint of numismatists, horses and the
REME. He was counsellor to Dagobert I, Merovingian
King of France in the seventh century and said to
be a very comely man with rosy cheeks, girlish hair
and lovely long fingers. On the instructions of Babo
the Treasurer, he crafted two gorgeous thrones from
an amount of gold that would normally only have
provided for one and for this was made a bishop. He is
best known for having miraculously shoed a stubborn
horse, by cutting its leg off, sticking on a horseshoe, and
reattaching it to the chastened beast.

St Marcian of Constantinople

He was born to a noble and wealthy family in the fifth century but eschewed the world and its pomps to be ordained priest and eventually became the Treasurer of the great cathedral of Hagia Sophia in Constantinople. He had a tremendous flair for design and was always giving it, and other churches, makeovers. Personally he was rather austere, giving all his wealth away, fasting rigorously, and basing his life on that of John the Baptist, of whom he was very fond. One day, vested as a priest in the gorgeous robes he had designed for the cathedral, he came across a beggar, naked and wretched in the street, so he stopped and gave him everything he was wearing except for his chasuble, the richly embroidered garment a priest wears at the altar. It was so richly embroidered that when he arrived at the cathedral the Patriarch rebuked him for dressing so flamboyantly. Marcian, with a flourish, took off his chasuble and revealed his nakedness to the Patriarch and congregation. Clergy might like to try this as part of a stewardship drive in their own parishes. St Marcian is now the patron saint of strippers.

St Daniel of Constantinople

He was a fifth-century monk who one day encountered St Simeon the Stylite. Simeon lived alone on top of a pillar. Daniel was so impressed he built his own pillar near Constantinople and went up it. Unfortunately he had not sought planning permission, so the authorities sent for the patriarch to get him down. Daniel refused, but the patriarch ordained him a priest against his will, by shouting the liturgy at the top of his voice. He then had someone bring a ladder and climbed up it with the Eucharist so Daniel could give him communion. Daniel stood on top of his pillar for 33 years, never coming down, standing for many hours until he collapsed, exhausted. As a result his feet covered with terrible sores, and he was naked thanks to high winds from Thrace which stripped him of his clothes. At least two Emperors came to see him and ask him theological questions and he gave one a good ear bashing about monophysitism. He was also good at predicting fires.

St Luke the Wonder-Worker

He grew up on a farm in tenth-century Thessalonia, so pious a child he drove everyone mad. He kept giving his clothes away to beggars and often walked around naked and became very skinny from sharing his food with the poor. He also sowed seed intended for his father's fields on the fields of others, and although his own fields miraculously yielded an abundant harvest, his father grew so cross Luke ran away to join a monastery. Unfortunately he was captured by Roman soldiers who thought he was an escaped slave and eventually sent him home. He became terribly ascetic, sleeping in a trench to remind him of the grave and going without food or water. One day an angel visited him and let a hook down through his open mouth into his insides and 'drew out a certain fleshly member therefrom'. Thereafter he was untroubled by the desires of the flesh. Then he met some monks travelling to Athens and went with them to their monastery where he was admitted as a novice, but unfortunately his mother appeared in a vision to the abbot and insisted he send Luke home again. Eventually she relented and aged eighteen he built a hermitage where he became famous for levitating.

St Eulalia

A terribly devout girl who lived at the time of the fourth-century persecutions of Christians. She was so keen on achieving martyrdom that her mother imprisoned her in the countryside, but Eulalia ran away to Emerita and insisted on appearing in court before the prefect Dacian. There she danced around, sticking her tongue out and said such rude things about the pagan gods and the Emperor that Dacian sentenced her to death, though he did try to bribe her to shut up first. She was tortured, then burnt at the stake, all the while mocking her executioners, and at the moment of her death a white dove flew out of her mouth and snow fell to cover her nakedness. This so frightened the soldiers they all ran away.

St Nicholas

He was Bishop of Myra in the fourth century and a remarkable thaumaturge. He resurrected three little boys who had been murdered, chopped and pickled to be sold as ham by a wicked butcher, and saved three girls from being sold into prostitution by filling their stockings, found drying over a fire, with three bags of gold which he chucked through a window – the origin of the three golden balls in the sign of a pawnbroker, for whom Nicholas is patron (as well as children, the wrongly accused and bishops). His bones, which were divided between the Italian cities of Venice and Bari, were subjected to scientific analysis recently and it was discovered that he looked like Ronnie Corbett with a broken nose. He visited my church to give bags of gold coins to our Beavers, Cubs, Rainbows, Brownies and our server Cory, who forgot himself for a moment.

St Valentine of Terni and

Probably the best-known feast day in the whole saintly calendar is 14 February, but confusingly it celebrates two saints with the same name. St Valentine of Terni and St Valentine of Rome were third-century Christians who both met sticky ends, martyred for the faith: Valentine of Terni, a bishop, was arrested by the prefect Placidius who had him scourged before beheading him; and Valentine of Rome, a physician, was thrown in a dungeon but converted his jailer by restoring the sight of his daughter.

St Valentine of Rome

This very much displeased the emperor, Claudius the Goth, who had Valentine of Rome beaten with clubs before being beheaded and had the jailer and his family executed too. How these tales came to be associated with love and romance is difficult to ascertain, but it is thought that the feast coincided with the Roman Lupercalia festival on the Ides of February, when boys would draw the names of eligible girls in honour of the goddess Juno. The Saints Valentine, probably the same person, are portrayed in art as bishops with epileptics at their feet, reproving idolaters, and sometimes with a pet cockerel. Valentine is patron of beekeepers and is invoked against swooning.

Blessed Marcolino of Forli

He was born in Italy in the fourteenth century and joined the Dominican order when he was only ten. The Dominicans, the Order of Preachers, have a notably active apostolate, but Marcolino was a contemplative, so absorbed in the adoration of Our Lord and Our Lady that his brethren thought he was half asleep or dim-witted. It was only when one of them overheard him conversing with Our Lady, who kindly replied, that they realised what was going on. He was, one said, 'a stranger on earth, concerned only with the things of heaven.' He died aged eighty, and a beautiful child appeared in the streets of the town crying 'The saintly friar is dead!' and disappeared.

St Pratt

He and his brother St Hyacinth lived in the third century and were PAs to the cross-dressing St Eugenia. They converted her to Christianity but were unable to stop her pretending to be a man – she once appeared dressed as an abbot in front of her own father, a judge. In the end all three were martyred, scourged and beheaded, and Pratt's relics show signs of having been burned too. For some utterly mysterious reason the parish church of Blisland in Cornwall is dedicated to Pratt and Hyacinth. It nestles in the lee of Brown Willy and its jolly vicar, Canon Sherry Bryan, leads her flock in procession on St Pratt's Day, 11 September.

St Theodore and

Saints Theodore and Theophanes were brothers and Graptoi. They were born in Moab in the late eighth century and became monks of St Sabas in Jerusalem. Famed for their brilliance and piety they were persecuted by the Byzantine Emperor for their devotion to the veneration of sacred images during the Iconoclastic Controversy. They were banished to a ghastly island in the Black Sea and on their release went to Constantinople where they refused even to talk to the iconoclasts. For this, the Emperor Theophilus ordered a 12-line iambic verse to be cut into the flesh of their faces.

St Theophanes

It read: 'These men have appeared at Jerusalem as vessels full of the iniquity of superstitious error, and were driven thence for their crimes. Having fled to Constantinople, they forsook not their impiety. Wherefore they have been banished from thence and thus stigmatised on their faces.' It took two days to cut this into their flesh, and so they became Graptoi, 'the written-upon'. Today, of course, the popularity of tattooing has turned many into Graptoi, although their defacement is generally elected.

St Bibiana

Her parents, Flavian and Dafrosa of Acquapendente, fell victim to the persecution of Emperor Julian the Apostate and Bibiana and her sister Demetria were turned over to a dreadful woman called Rufina, who locked them up in a mad house and tried to groom them for her own gratification. It was all too much for Demetria, who dropped down dead, but Bibiana refused to submit and was eventually scourged to death with plumb lines. A church was built over her grave and in its garden there grew a herb which proved efficacious in the treatment of cerebral crises. She is patron of epileptics.

Blessed Maurice of Hungary

It is said that the night sky was lit with portentous stars at the birth of this fourteenth-century prince. He was rather a fey and dreamy child, who liked dressing up and playing church in the castle chapel. An old friar predicted he would live a life dedicated to God, but when his parents died young he inherited great wealth and status and was obliged to marry. It was a white marriage, believe it or not, and his wife, the daughter of the Count Palatine, couldn't be bothered with it really and went off to be a nun which so annoyed her father he had Maurice kidnapped and shut up in a tower. It made no difference and in the end he let him go and Maurice spent the next 30 years as a Dominican friar, eschewing his throne to become 'a zealous addict of poverty', wearing the shabbiest habit and living in the dreariest cell.

He became so holy that at night rooms lit up whenever he entered them and locked doors would swing wide open to let him through. Contemporary Dominican friars, while holy, are obliged to use light switches and keys to go about their business.

St Bademus of Persia

A fourth-century monk, he founded the Abbey of
Bethlapeta in Persia where he lived a life of great
austerity and holiness. Unfortunately he fell foul of King
Shapur who had him thrown into prison with seven
of his brethren where they were whipped daily for 120
days. Prince Nersan, a Persian convert to Christianity,
was also subjected to this treatment but found it so
disagreeable he renounced his faith. The king promised
him his freedom if he would execute Bademus with his
own hand. Nersan took the sword but was so weedy he
just poked Bademus a bit until the saint grew impatient
and told him to get on with it. Eventually Nersan
managed to deal a fatal blow but to no avail. King
Shapur had him tortured and executed too. The Persian
church has suffered much persecution but continues
today under the Patriarchate of Mar Dinkha IV.

St Aurea the Anchoress

She was born in Moorish Spain in the eleventh century and when she was aged nine decided she had tired of the world, and applied to the monastery of San Millán de la Cogolla for assistance in withdrawing from it. The Abbot built a cell for her in the wall of the monastery church, a narrow space with a tiny window giving a view of the altar, and a little hatch through which the necessities of life could pass to and fro. She was then consecrated and walled up in it, and thus became an anchoress, a vocation which may strike us as rather extreme, but was very popular with holy women in the Middle Ages. Aurea adored her new life and took to it with tremendous relish. After ten years her favourite saints, Eulalia, Agatha, and Cecilia appeared to her in a vision and threw her onto a comfy bed as a foretaste of her suffering and death.

Eulalia then gave her a talking pigeon for a pet, which instructed her in the elements of Christian discipleship. To pass the time she embroidered gorgeous vestments, before catching something horrible and dying, very contented, at the age of twenty-seven. She is venerated to this day with a Spanish version of morris dancing.

Sts Simeon Barsabae

April 21st is the Feast of Sts Simeon Barsabae and
companions. Saint Simeon was made Metropolitan
of Persia after the Council of Nicea in 325 but got
into trouble when cruel King Shapur (his wickedness,
passim) found out he was writing long chatty letters to
the Roman Emperor Constantius II and rather insisted
he became a Zoroastrian, like Freddy Mercury.
Simeon refused, though swore loyalty to the
Persian throne.

and companions

Unfortunately this was not enough for the king, who imprisoned and tortured him and then, on Good Friday, obliged him to witness the beheading of Abdechalas, Ananias, Usthazanes, Pusicius and ninety-five others, before he was beheaded himself. You'd think this would be enough for King Shapur, but no, he also accused Simeon's sister Pherbutha and two of her friends of witchcraft and had them sawn in half. Here is Shapur going about his wickedness.

Blessed Thora of Pisa

She was born in 1362, the daughter of the chief magistrate. She was a pious child but was nevertheless married off at thirteen. Her young husband soon died of plague and she fled to a convent but her father sent her brothers round and she was forcibly removed and imprisoned at the family's palazzo where she was kept confined for five months, unable to receive communion. One day, Catherine of Siena was passing through Pisa, so her father asked her to talk some sense into Thora; but instead she strengthened her resolve and in the end her father relented and built her her own convent. It was terribly strict, austere, and rigorous, and no men were allowed inside. This led to a terrible tragedy. In the febrile politics of fourteenth-century Pisa, her father was betrayed by a friend, fell from favour and was lynched by a mob outside the very convent he had built for Thora. Her brothers were there too and piteously cried to be given sanctuary from the mob, but Thora said she was terribly sorry but they couldn't come in. They pleaded with her as the mob encircled them but it seems the lady was not for turning, and she watched from a window as her brothers were torn to pieces. In spite of these controversies, after her death her body was placed in a coffin with great pomp and ceremony, and installed under the altar in her convent's church. Ever since that day, when a sister is approaching death, Thora's bones rattle noisily in her coffin as a portent.

St Veronica

According to tradition, she wiped the face of Jesus with her veil as he bore the cross on which he was to die to Golgotha. His face left its imprint on the cloth, called the Veronica (meaning true likeness), and in a striking display of magnanimity cured the Emperor Tibierus, tristissimus hominum, of sickness. It soon became one of the most precious relics in Christendom, able to cure blindness, ague and to slake the thirst of anyone who sucked it. Versions of it are said to be held now by St Peter's in Rome, the Hofburg Palace in Vienna, the Monastery of the Holy Face in Alicante, Jaén Cathedral in Spain, the church of the Holy Face in Genoa, the chapel of San Silvestro in Rome and in the little Capuchin monastery of Manopello in Italy. It also gives its name to the first pass of the cape used by matadors in a bullfight.

Blessed Clement of Dunblane

It seemed appropriate that the new Pope Francis chose to be inaugurated on 19 March, the day the Church throughout the world remembers Blessed Clement of Dunblane. He, like Francis, was a member of a religious order, the Dominicans in his case, and was in 1233 the first to be made bishop in Scotland, taking a new broom to sorry circumstances. The Church in Scotland at that time had rather fallen into the hands of careerists and politicians, its revenues misappropriated, its governance in stagnation, its clergy in disarray. Clement with great skill succeeded in putting it on a sounder footing, wresting control of its revenues from the worldly and preposterous, giving it new energy through honest preaching, restoring the liturgy where it had lapsed into emptiness and show, and encouraging the clergy to live more faithfully as Christ lived.

Laudare!
Benedicere!
Praedicare!

St Margaret of Hungary

In 1245, aged four, she was given to a convent by her father, King Béla IV, as a thank you to God for having delivered his realm from the Mongol horde. She lived with the Dominican sisters on Rabbit Island and insisted on wearing a hair shirt, a girdle made of iron and shoes spiked on the inside, performing the dirtiest and most menial jobs, so dirty that her Sisters would not come near her for she smelled so awful. For dynastic reasons her father tried to marry her to King Ottakar II of Bohemia but she would have none of it and set about performing splendid miracles, 74 of them, including stopping a flood which threatened the city of Budapest, making some jolly friars stay the night by summoning a terrific rainstorm, and restoring to life a maid who had absentmindedly fallen down a well. St Elizabeth of Hungary was her auntie, by the way. She died aged only twenty-eight and is patroness of the malodorant.

St Benen of Armagh

He was the son of a fifth-century Meath chieftain and was baptised as a boy by St Patrick. After the ceremony Patrick fell asleep and Benen noticed his robes smelled unpleasant and were infested with creepy crawlies so he picked wild flowers and scattered them over the saint's sleeping form. When he woke and saw what had happened Patrick said, 'He's a good boy.' Benen stowed away in his chariot and, when discovered, insisted St Patrick take him with him. He became St Patrick's personal psalm-singer, following him everywhere singing hymns in a lovely light tenor and was so adored by St Patrick he turned him into a bambi to escape the death-dealing guards of the high king Laoghaire. Benen is the patron saint of air freshener.

St Derfel

He was a knight of King Arthur and a tremendous fighter but after the Battle of Camlan, where King Arthur was killed, he laid down his arms and became a hermit, living in a cave at what is now Llanderfel in Merionethshire. Its church, which he founded, had a lovely statue of him riding a horse carved from wood and it attracted pilgrims in their hundreds, drawn – it is said – by its miraculous power to deliver the damned from hell.

As you can imagine this went down very badly with Thomas Cromwell as he went around the country vandalising churches for Henry VIII. He ordered the saint to be dehorsed and sent to London and used as firewood for the burning of heretics, but the locals tried everything to stop him for they believed in the ancient prophecy that the statue 'should set a whole forest afire'. It was taken to Smithfield, chopped into pieces, and used to burn to ashes the Catholic priest, John Forest. Prophecy fulfilled.

St Sergius and

They were soldiers and, some have suggested, lovers in fourth-century Syria. Roman citizens, they served as officers in Caesar Galerius Maximianus's army and were inseparable. One day he asked them to come on a day out to the pagan temple, but they refused to enter; he realised they were secret Christians and lost his temper. He dressed them up as ladies, paraded them around and everyone mocked them in falsetto. Bacchus was then beaten to death and the next day his spirit appeared to Sergius beseeching him to hold fast, and that they would soon be together forever, in the words of the Rick Astley song.

St Bacchus

Sergius was then brutally tortured and eventually murdered but did not renounce the faith. They became immensely popular after their martyrdom and the hagiographies make such mention of their closeness, even describing them as εραϲται, which can mean 'lovers', that the controversial American scholar John Boswell has suggested they were joined to one another by the rite of αδελπηοποιεϲιϲ, 'brother-making', which he argues was a sort of early same-sex blessing.

St Enda of Aranmore

He was a particularly bloodthirsty Irish warrior of the sixth century, who one day returning from battle decided to call in on his sister, the Abbess Fanchea, at her convent. His soldiers were singing riotously and rattling their weapons which disturbed the nuns. Fanchea was sent for and seeing her brother's hands crimson and smoking with the blood of the slain, she rebuked him and said if he mended his ways she would give him her comeliest novice for a wife. He agreed, but when he asked to see his bride Fanchea took him to see a corpse instead which obliged him to reflect on the transitory nature of life. So he became a monk and went off to found the great monastic community on the Isles of Aran, the 'Sun of the West', according to St Columba.

It was incredibly austere, the monks living in dripping caves without heating or comforts of any kind. Enda wrought miracles, like making the feet of a rival stick in the sand so he could not move, and keeping in a silken purse a magic stone given to St Brendan the Navigator by a dwarf. It floats on water and is set with a gem which points to the Last Isle of the West, very handy for navigation in the days before GPS. St Enda was a great favourite of those with nationalist sympathies in nineteenth-century Ireland and he gave his name to a school where the Irish language, arts and modes of dress were cultivated.

St Longinus the Centurion

He was the Roman soldier who attended the crucifixion, pierced Christ's side with a lance, and acknowledged him as the Son of God. Cineastes will remember John Wayne playing this part in 'The Greatest Story Ever Told'. According to legend, the sight of this humiliation blinded him, but sight was restored by the blood pouring from Christ's side. He converted, resigned his commission, and became a monk in Cappadocia.

He got into trouble with the governor for his faith and one day smashed up with a hammer idols, from which devils escaped and possessed, enraged and blinded the governor. Longinus said he was sorry about that, and only his own death would restore his sight. The governor crossly put him to torture and then had him executed, which indeed restored his vision. The governor also converted, Longinus's martyred soul went straight to heaven, and everyone else went home. During the first crusade his lance was discovered in a church in Antioch and his cult became terribly popular for a while. It ended up in Mantua where it was displayed with the Holy Sponge.

St Waldebert

A noble Frankish soldier who had an epiphany one day and surrendered to a monastery his weapons and armour, which zoomed up to the roof of the church and hung there of their own accord. He went to live in a hole in the ground but after a while the monks made him abbot and he reorganised them, securing advantageous tax breaks with the revenue, and in a succession of canny deals greatly extending their property portfolio. He was marvellous with animals, and once scolded a gaggle of wild geese for pecking up the crops and made them stand in a corner until they were sorry. While they were expiating their sins a monk sneaked up and took one for the cooking pot. The remaining geese complained about this to Waldebert so he said a prayer and the cooked and eaten bits of goose were sicked up by the monks and reconstituted themselves into the living animal. He also had a magic wooden bowl which cured the poorly, well into the tenth century.

St John of Capistrano

A soldier saint and of one of the nastiest saints of all. Born in the kingdom of Naples in the fourteenth century he trained as a lawyer and became Governor of Perugia, then at war with nearly everybody. Taken prisoner by Sigismondo Pandolfo Malatesta, he had an intense conversion experience in jail and on his release abandoned his wife and joined the Franciscans. He became a tremendous ascetic, preaching fire and brimstone to such effect he became famous throughout Europe, once in Brescia keeping a crowd of 126,000 enthralled. I'm sorry to say much of his preaching was condemnatory of the Jewish people; indeed, he was so virulently and violently anti-Semitic that he became known as the Scourge of the Jews. He mustered a fleet for the pope to exile all the Jews of the papal states and in southern Germany so inflamed the Christian populations that Jews were expelled and even burned at the stake for heresy. He also persecuted ruthlessly the Hussites, who were very influential in the later rise of Protestantism. In 1456, at the invitation of the pope, he raised an army and, aged seventy, led it into battle against the Turks besieging Belgrade. He was victorious but caught bubonic plague from infected mercenaries and died at Ilok in what is now Croatia. Seventy years later, Calvin had his relics thrown down a well.

St Catherine of Siena

She was one of the greatest saints of the Church, the most marvellously passionate Dominican nun who received the stigmata from holy rays emanating from a crucifix. She ate nothing but the Blessed Sacrament for eight years (in the end it used to jump out of the hand of the priest and fly of its own accord into her mouth), levitate so buoyantly it was as if she was filled with helium, and fall into the kitchen fire during ecstasies but emerge from it unharmed. So spectacular was her holiness that she became the confidante of popes and kings and wrote a correspondence which remains one of the highest achievements of early Tuscan literature.

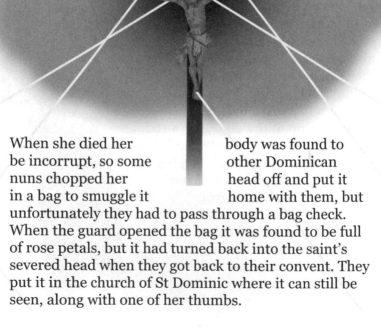

When she died her body was found to be incorrupt, so some other Dominican nuns chopped her head off and put it in a bag to smuggle it home with them, but unfortunately they had to pass through a bag check. When the guard opened the bag it was found to be full of rose petals, but it had turned back into the saint's severed head when they got back to their convent. They put it in the church of St Dominic where it can still be seen, along with one of her thumbs.

St Wilfrid of Ripon

He was an exceptionally worldly bishop who rather scandalised the Venerable Bede with his love of pomp and show. As Abbot of Ripon he was of the victorious party at the Synod of Whitby which sought to impose Roman norms on the English Church, then in thrall to liturgical dance, improvisational wailing, bird watching and other Celtic customs. He was promised the See of York but someone else sneaked in before he got there. He got the Archbishop of Canterbury to restore him and immediately set about obliging choirs in his churches to sing dignified plainsong. He also kept a retinue of warriors who would kidnap boys with nice voices, but he was then deposed again and ended up in exile in Sussex. He was constantly complaining to the pope in Rome, the first English bishop to do this, and eventually all his rights and privileges were restored to him. He celebrated this by building gorgeous churches with fancy continental flourishes, like glazed windows and porches. He adorned them with gold and purple furnishings, silks and jewelled Gospel books, and kept filling them up with relics he obtained on his trips to Rome. He died in the pretty Northamptonshire town of Oundle, famous for its public school, where Professor Dawkins first acquired his distaste for the blandishments of religion.

Padre Pio

Born in 1887 to peasant
farmers in Campania he
suffered spectacular ill health
as a child and conversed quite
happily with Jesus and Mary
who appeared to him in visions. He
became a friar in the Capuchin order,
which gives its name to the cappuccino.
He continued in ill health, suffering loss of
appetite, insomnia, exhaustion, fainting spells,
migraine, asthmatic bronchitis, a kidney stone,
abdominal pain, gastritis, rhinitis, chronic otitis,
pulmonary tuberculosis, a cyst, a malignant tumour,
exudative pleuritis and arthritis. He also made strange
noises through the night, was often seen to have
suffered bruises which he said were the result of
brawling with the devil, and was reported to levitate
by one of his brethren. He then experienced the
transreverberation of the soul – pierced by a fiery dart
of divine love – and received the stigmata, the marks of
the wounds of Christ. These excited controversy and his
critics accused him inflicting the wounds with carbolic
acid and faking the odour of sanctity with cologne. The
evidence for this, however, is slight and contradictory
and he became terribly famous and adored. He had the
gift of prophecy and told a young priest who came to see
him he would rise to the highest office in the Church –
he later became John Paul II. On the day of his death
in 1968 a lady in Venezuela called Maria Esperanza de
Bianchini reported that Padre Pio appeared to her in
a vision and stated 'I have come to say good bye. My
time has come. It is your turn.' Her husband was then
confronted by the tricky spectacle of her face morphing
into that of the bearded friar. Next thing, she was
levitating during Mass and bilocating too.

St Margaret of Cortona

A thirteenth-century Italian floozie, she escaped the loveless house of her stepmother when she was eighteen to run away with a nobleman. He promised to marry her, but did not, and for nine years she lived in his castle, dressed in gaudy silks and glittering jewels and went about arrogantly singing songs to herself in a high pitched voice and laughing at the degradations of the poor. She bore him a son, but one day his little dog bade her follow him to an oak tree in the forest where she found, to her horror, her lover's murdered and disfigured body. It was so unsightly she renounced the pleasures of the flesh there and then, but was thrown out of the castle and reduced to penury anyway. Her stepmother refused to have her back, on grounds of her notoriety, even though she walked round Cortona with a rope around her neck saying she was very sorry for having been such a strumpet. She ended up, after some controversy, in the care of the Franciscans, where she became extremely austere and pious, experiencing ecstasies in which she would mortify her own flesh so severely her friends staged an intervention. In the end she became highly skilled at intervening to alleviate the suffering of souls in purgatory and was often visited by spectral figures who would ask if she could kindly give them a helping hand to heaven. When she died they turned up and formed an honour guard for the ascent of her own soul to heaven. She is patroness of floozies, strumpets, sex addicts and third children.

St Gertrude the Great

An orphan in thirteenth-century Thuringia, she joined the Benedictine convent at Helfta where she excelled as a scholar before experiencing an intense religious ecstasy. Jesus came to her and laid her head on his breast so she could hear his heart beating. Another time, during Holy Communion, Jesus appeared and draped her sisters in beautiful white robes glittering with violet jewels that gave off the smell of Timotei shampoo. In art St Gertrude is often shown wearing the white habit of a Cistercian and holding an Abbess's crosier. She was neither a Cistercian nor an abbess. And she was never formally canonised but was equipollently stuck in the Roman Martyrology by Pope Clement XII.

St Frances of Rome

She was born to a noble family in the fourteenth century and wanted to be a nun but her parents forced her to marry the commander of the papal troops when she was only twelve. Fortunately he was away a lot fighting wars and she could sit quietly at home having ecstasies. One day their son was kidnapped by Neapolitan soldiers but Frances prayed to Our Lady and the horse they'd put him on refused to budge so they gave him back. Her husband eventually died so Frances went about the city doing good works, having visions and founding a confraternity of pious matrons.

At night she was preceded on her travels by an angel shining a mysterious light and for this reason in 1925 Pope Pius XI declared her patroness of motoring.

St Giovanna Marie Bonomo

She was a nun of the Poor Clares in seventeenth-century Italy. She was a great one for falling into ecstasies, indeed she fell into one during her own profession which greatly irked all the other novices who felt the special day was being rather hijacked. This pattern continued in the convent and many of her sisters though she was, at best, an attention seeker, at worst, a heretic and they bitterly persecuted her by shutting up when she came into the room, hiding her prayer book and sticking their tongues out at her behind her back. Like many blessed with spectacular piety, agreement about her holiness only emerged after she died.

St Elvis

He was a sixth-century Irish bishop, best known for having baptised St David. The illegitimate child of the King of Munster and a slave girl, he very nearly didn't survive infancy, for the King refused to acknowledge him and ordered him be smothered. The man charged with this heinous act gave him to a she-wolf instead, who raised him.

Eventually he was taken in by some Britons and ended up in Rome where he was consecrated a bishop and sent back to Ireland. There, one day, a hunt passed by pursuing an old she-wolf who ran to Elvis and laid her head upon his breast. It was his foster mother, who lived with him thereafter. Just before he died he was picked up by a magical ship which took him on a tour during which he learned the secret of his death. He is the patron saint of wolves and hound dogs.

St Francis of Paola

Born in the fifteenth century in the Kingdom of Naples.
The patron saint of vegans, he was a total darling. He
was afflicted by a mysterious swelling but nevertheless
joined the Franciscans. However he found community
life was not for him and sought solitude in a cave. There
he was joined by followers so he founded an order of
Franciscan hermits – the Minim Friars. They lived an
austere life with a particular discipline of eschewing all
animal products. Francis adored all God's creatures, but
his best friend was a trout called Antonella who lived
in a pool. One day a priest saw her and thought she
would make a tasty lunch so he caught Antonella, took
her home, and tossed her into a frying pan. St Francis
discovered the priest half way through his lunch and
berated him for eating his friend. The priest threw what
was left of her at the saint and went off in a huff. St
Francis gathered the pieces of fried fish and returned
them to the pool with a prayer. Antonella immediately
became whole and swam around joyously, singing a
hymn. In later life he developed formidable powers and
was able to zoom around the Straits of Messina on his
cloak admonishing potentates and raising the dead.

St Kenny

Born to a minstrel in sixth-century Ireland, he became a monk and went as a missionary to the Western Isles of Scotland. He was a tremendous preacher and would glow like a firework when he got to a good bit of his sermon.

He lived part of his life as a hermit communing with nature. Once some mice, described as 'naughty', gnawed his sandals, so he cursed them and they all jumped into the sea. Another time some birds were squawking so much they put him off his book so he made them all have a lie-down until he'd finished. He also used a tame stag's antlers as a book rest, although one day it ran away before he'd finished his chapter. It came back eventually without having lost his place. Many places in western Scotland are named after him, like the island of Inch Kenneth.

St Basil the Younger

He was rather a dear, a hermit who lived near
Constantinople in the tenth century. As a young man
he went to live in a forest where he ran about in rags
whooping which so alarmed some civil servants, who
were passing, that they had him arrested and hauled
before Salmon the Patriarch. Unimpressed by the
wicked Patriarch, Basil refused to tell him who he was
or what he was doing, even under torture. Salmon first
had him suspended upside down for three days, but this
did not work. He had him thrown to a lion, but the lion
just rolled over at his feet so Basil
could tickle its tummy.

Then he had him thrown in the sea, but he was rescued
by two dolphins who carried him to the shore. In the
end Salmon gave up and Basil lived very happily,
healing the sick and berating aristocratic strumpets, to
the age of one hundred and ten.

St Edmund

He was the king of East Anglia in the ninth century and rather a dear. A German, he came to Hunstanton when he was fourteen and found himself proclaimed sovereign, then crowned on Christmas Day in Suffolk. He then went back to Hunstanton and sat in a tower learning the psalms. He was a just and wise ruler and was said to be unmoved by flatterers. Unfortunately East Anglia was being ravaged by Vikings at the time and the Great Heathen Army invaded. He put up a stout fight but eventually the Vikings chased him to Hoxne in Suffolk where he hid under a bridge. There was a wedding happening in Hoxne that day and as the bride and groom crossed the bridge they saw Edmund's spurs glittering and waved to him which sadly gave away his hiding place to Ivar the Boneless. Ivar insisted he renounce the faith, Edmund refused, so he was beaten, shot with arrows until he looked 'like a hedgehog', and finally beheaded. They threw his head into the forest and when his followers went to look for it they discovered a wolf shouting, 'Hic! Hic! Hic!' (Here! Here! Here!) holding the king's head in its paws. The body was buried but when exhumed, to be moved to a special tomb at Bury, the arrow wounds had healed and his severed head had miraculously become reattached to his body. He is the patron saint of pandemics.

St William Firmatus

He was a French doctor who lived in Tours in the eleventh century but became so disgusted with the inequitable economics of the healthcare sector that he moved in with his mother, gave his possessions away to the poor, and eventually went to live in a hermitage near Laval, occasionally wandering around striking the ground with his staff to create springs. He was adored by animals and liked to sit by a pond near his cell chatting to the fish who would came and sit on his knee with no ill effects. On cold days little birds would zoom into his trousers to warm up, but he could be stern too. A naughty wild boar was trampling the crops so he made it go on a fast in a lonely cave. When William died there was, unfortunately, a tremendous row over who should have his relics and in the end they were secured by the town of Mortain which sent in a snatch squad of combat-ready clergy which took them by force. Mortain, I'm sorry to say, was all but destroyed in 1944 by the US 30th Infantry Division when it engaged the German counter offensive in Operation Lüttich. J. D. Salinger was there and never really recovered.

St Kieran

He was one of the Twelve Apostles of Ireland, Bishop of
Saigir, and sometimes confused with St Piran, Patron of
Cornwall, whose feast falls on the same day, 5 March.
Kieran was born in County Cork in the sixth century
after a star fell into his mother's mouth, which a druid
interpreted as a good portent. He must have rather
disappointed her at first, for he took to living in the
woods dressed in animal skins with a wolf, a badger
and a fox helping him build little follies. The fox kept
stealing his shoes, but the badger retrieved them and
the fox was scolded and eventually repented. One day
St Patrick turned up and Kieran was made a bishop.
He was very good at working miracles. He raised little
birds from the dead and once killed the Lord Justice of
Ireland by making Athlone Castle fall on him.

Blessed Ambrose Sansedoni

He was born in 1220 with twisted arms and legs and screamed constantly so his mother gave him away to a nurse. She discovered that he would become calm near relics, but nevertheless in church she covered his hideous face with a cloth. A pilgrim told her not to, for the child's face would 'one day be the glory of the city'. The baby then said the word 'Jesus' and stretched out his limbs which miraculously grew straight. At the age of two he was getting up in the middle of the night to pray and read from Lives of the Saints and when he was seventeen he became a Dominican friar. At first he wanted to be a scholar, but Thomas Aquinas put him off and he became a famous mystic instead. While deep in mystic prayer a shaft of brilliant light would suffuse him and he would rise slowly into the air which would throng with gaudy parrots.

St Hugh of Lincoln

A twelth-century English bishop and rebuilder of Lincoln Cathedral. He once bit a finger off the preserved arm of Mary Magdalene while staying with some monks in France and took it home. He later made friends with a swan.

St Richard of Chichester

He was one of the greatest of English saints. He was born in Droitwich in 1197 and was a terribly pious child, going to Mass daily and giving little sermons aged five. Orphaned early, the family estates passed to his ne'er-do-well brother who managed them so poorly Richard had to till the land himself. A brilliant student, he went to the universities of Oxford and Paris to study. In Paris he shared digs with two others and they lived austerely on porridge, so poor they shared one coat between three. He became a parson in Deal, but in 1244, after a tremendous row, he was consecrated Bishop of Chichester. He lived very simply, begging a living, and used to get up very early and wandered through his monks' dormitories urging them all to wake up too. He also insisted they dressed like clergymen and took a dim view of clerical ribaldry. Most notable, however, was his commitment to the poor. 'It will never do,' he said, 'to eat out off gold and silver plates and bowls, while Christ is suffering in the person of His poor,' and he gave away nearly all his wealth, personal and episcopal, as alms.

Let his improving example remind us of our own obligations to the poor and of the desirability of appointing leaders who know what it is to be poor themselves, particularly when their policies risk reducing others to penury. Pleasingly, but mysteriously, he is patron of the Milanese coachmen's guild and wrote one of the songs for the musical 'Godspell'.

St Cerbonius

He was bishop of Populonia during the Barbarian invasions of the sixth centuruy. The faithful of Populonia, notorious slugabeds, got annoyed with his habit of rising very early to say Mass at daybreak and complained to Pope Vigilius. The pope sent his legate to scold him and when he arrived he found Cerbonius eating breakfast which the legate falsely thought to be before Mass, a dangerous heresy, although Cerbonius had actually already said Mass. He was arrested and conveyed to Rome but on the way he miraculously tamed some wild geese which flew along with him doing aerial stunts. When he got there Cerbonius insisted on rousing the pope at daybreak and asked him if he heard angels singing. The Pope said actually yes he did, and allowed Cerbonius to say Mass as early as he pleased before going back to sleep. Cerbonius was then nearly eaten by a bear, but it fell over.

Our Lady of Walsingham

In 1061 the Blessed Virgin Mary appeared in a vision to the Lady Richeldis at Walsingham which is near Wells-next-the-Sea in Norfolk. Mary asked Richeldis to build a replica of the simple wooden shack she'd lived in – the Holy House – which she did. A shrine was built around it and it became a great centre for pilgrimage, known as 'England's Nazareth'. Among those who visited were Henry III, Edward II, Edward III, Henry IV, Edward IV, Henry VII, and Henry VIII. Unfortunately by then it had become notorious for the laxity of its clergy and the brutality of its Prior, and despite efforts at reform it was suppressed in 1538, when 'the image of Our Lady of Walsingham was brought up to London with all the jewels that hung around it at the King's commandment, and divers other images, both in England and Wales, that were used for common pilgrimage ... and they were burnt at Chelsea by my Lord Privy Seal'. The buildings were pulled down and the shrine desecrated, but 400 years later the great Anglo-Catholic priest, Fr Alfred Hope Patten SSC, restored it. In 1931 a new Holy House was dedicated and Mary's statue reinstated. Walsingham is again a centre for pilgrimage and a sort of headquarters for Anglo Catholics, though Roman Catholics maintain a chapel there too, and the Orthodox recently converted the tiny railway station into the Church of St Seraphim and gave it a charming onion dome.

The Discovery of the True Cross

St Helena was an Essex girl and mother of the Emperor Constantine. In 335, when she was eighty, she went on a trip to Jerusalem and decided to build a church on the hill of Calvary where the crucifixion took place, but no one was sure exactly where. She had her suspicions about a pagan temple, had it razed, and there found a hole with three identical crosses in it. Christ's had been labelled but the label had fallen off so the Bishop suggested she wave them over a poorly old lady to see if one made her perk up; one did, and the True Cross was found. Bits of it went to Rome and were kept in the great church of Santa Croce, but most stayed in Jerusalem. So many chips were carved off and handed out to people to take home that the Reformer Calvin snorted through his moustaches that there were enough fragments of the True Cross knocking around to fill an entire ship. But in 1870 a Frenchman, Charles Rohault de Fleury, worked out that all the recorded fragments of the True Cross amounted to only 0.004 cubic metres of wood from a likely total of 0.178 cubic metres.

Our Lady of Good Counsel

Not a person, but a magic holy picture in Italy. The little town of Genazzano, near Rome, had given generously to Pope Sixtus to support the building of the great church of Santa Maria Maggiore, so he ordered a church to be built in the town as a thank you. On this day in 1467, as the townsfolk were celebrating the Octave of St Mark, the air was filled with exquisite music from whence no one knew and a mysterious cloud appeared and hovered around a bit before settling on the bare wall of the parish church. A great crowd gathered and the cloud disappeared revealing a lovely fresco, eighteen inches square and as thin as eggshell, showing the Virgin Mary and the Christ child. The Virgin Mary said, 'Hello, we have come from Albania,' and floated in mid-air for a while before sticking herself to the wall. So many miracles were performed in front of the picture that Pope Innocent XI stuck a crown on it, Pope Leo XIII endowed it with indulgences and Pope Pius XII placed his pontificate under the maternal care of Our Lady of Good Counsel.

St Theopompus

The Hieromartyr Theopompus was bishop of Nicomedia in the third century around the time of the persecution of the Roman Emperor Diocletian. So steadfast was the good bishop in proclaiming the faith he was brought before Diocletian himself, who commanded him to offer worship to the pagan god Apollo. Theopompus refused, so Diocletian had him thrown into a fiery furnace; but when the Emperor checked to see if the bishop had been reduced to ashes he found him quietly praying at the heart of the blaze, untouched by the flames. The Emperor commanded his sorcerer Theonas to make a deadly potion and gave it to the bishop to drink. Theopompus downed it one, smacked his lips and pronounced it delicious, whereupon Theonas proclaimed his own conversion to Christ. For this, Diocletian had him buried alive in a pit, while Theopompus was beheaded.

Sts Gwinear, Phiala and

Gwinear was a prince in fifth-century Ireland who had a mystic moment hunting one day with St Patrick and decided to renounce his worldly pomps and become a missionary. He took his sister Phiala and 769 others to evangelise the Celtic fringe.

their 769 companions

He wrought miracles, creating, for example, a drinking fountain for thirsty dogs and annoyed the wicked King Teudar of Cornwall, who liked to push Christians into a lake full of poisonous serpents. In the end, Gwinear and his companions surrendered themselves to Teudar's wrath and they were all beheaded at Hayle near Penzance.

St Spyridon

He was a Cypriot shepherd of the fourth century who one day managed to convince a pagan of the truth of the doctrine of the Trinity with a brick. Holding it up he said it was indeed a brick, but made of three constituents, earth, water and fire. The brick then burst into flame and squirted water everywhere, leaving Spyridon holding a handful of earth. For this he was made a bishop and attended the Council of Nicea in 325 where he took on Arius the Heresiarch. After his death Cyprus was invaded by the Moors, so his body was dug up, found to be undecayed, and sprouting fragrant basil – signs of sanctity. He was taken to Corfu, where his relics reside to this day, and are taken out for a grand procession on Palm Sunday to the accompaniment of the band of the Philharmonic Society of Corfu in gratitude for miraculously saving the island from the plague. If you ask they will show you the scratch marks in the rock where Spyridon finally prised the plague's talons away. He is patron of potters and the Tolstoy family too, who have a bit of him.

St Edward, King and Martyr

He was born in the tenth century, the son of King Edgar of England and a nun whom he had seduced. His uncertain parentage caused problems in the royal succession when Edgar died, with some supporting Edward, others his younger half brother Ethelred the Unready. Edward prevailed, but after his coronation everyone fell out. A comet appeared and there were 'manifold disturbances', including an unfortunate meeting at Calne when the floor of the room the court was meeting in collapsed and many were killed. In the end it got too much for Ethelred's mother, the Dowager Queen Elfrida, whom some thought a witch, so she invited him to Corfe Castle one day and while he drank the cup of welcome had him murdered. He was buried without ceremony, his remains lost. A thousand years later a skeleton was dug up by an archeologist called Wilson-Claridge and identified, in 1970, as King Edward's. He wanted to give the bones to Shaftesbury Abbey, but he fell out with his brother, who wanted them to go to the Russian Orthodox Church, so they ended up in a bank vault in Woking.

St Roderick and

Roderick was a Spanish priest living in Moorish Cordoba in the ninth century. Religious affairs were very complicated in Andalucía at that time and Roderick had one brother who was a lapsed Catholic and another who was a Muslim. These two got into a fight one day and Roderick tried to stop them, but as is so often the case where someone seeks to intervene in a religiously motivated row, they both turned on him and beat him up. The Muslim brother then had him hoisted on a litter and paraded round the town saying, 'He's a Muslim, he's a Muslim'.

St Solomon

Poor Roderick had passed out, but when he came to and realised what was happening, said 'No I'm not, no I'm not'. This came to the attention of the Qadi, a sort of Sharia magistrate, who asked him why he was denying he was a Muslim, but Roderick said he had never actually become a Muslim. Then Qadi didn't believe him and had him thrown into jail for apostasy. There he met a dear fellow called Solomon who had also been convicted of apostasy. They reportedly got on famously, but not for long. The Qadi had them both beheaded.

St Foy

St Foy was a virgin martyr of Aquitaine. She was much
given to miraculous japes, and once, when a faithless
man put a ring promised to her on his girlfriend's
finger, she caused it to swell agonisingly until the poor
girl blew her nose and it shot off at such a velocity it
made a hole in the floor. Foy fell foul of the Roman
authorities, who tried to martyr her by roasting her
to death on a red hot iron bed, but she kept creating
miraculous storms which put out the fire, so in the end
they beheaded her.

St Tetricus

He was the son of a bishop, Gregorius, and inherited his father's See when he died – not so unusual in the sixth century. Some questioned this, but during Tetricus's consecration the stone lid to his father's tomb miraculously rose to reveal the bishop's corpse smiling. However, Tetricus never quite managed to mollify his opponents, particularly his archdeacon, Raginfred, who lost his reason one day while out for a walk with his bishop. Tetricus sat down on a bench to grab forty winks but when he dozed off the archdeacon produced a sword and chopped his head off. This is neither the first nor last example of an archdeacon shortening a bishop's career.

St Idesbald of the Dunes

A twelfth-century scion of the noble house of Van der Gracht, he was a page boy and courtier to the Count of Flanders, much given to gaudy display, superciliousness and trivialities. One day he fancied a change so he went to the Abbey of Our Lady of the Dunes, a Cistercian monastery located in the sand hills between Dunkirk and Nieuwpoort, and asked if he might join. The monks said OK, and he did. To everyone's surprise the popinjay and fauntleroy impressed everyone with his piety and austerity and eventually became abbot.

There is a beer brewed in his honour, St Idesbald Blond, described thus: 'a typical standard Belgian blonde beer which pours a pale gold with a quite ferocious head. The nose is nothing to write home about and the flavour offers little distinguishable above a light fruity twang'. It is good, however, with fruits de mer.

St Dwynwen of Anglesey

Charming and comely, an ardent young fellow named Maelon demanded her hand in marriage. She refused and in answer to a prayer was handed a magic potion which she gave Maelon to drink and he turned to ice. Fortunately, in answer to some more prayers, he was miraculously defrosted. To avoid this happening again she became a nun and eventually the patron saint of Welsh lovers. Her motto was, 'nothing wins hearts like cheerfulness'. At the church dedicated to her in Llanddwyn there was a holy well with a fortune-telling fish in it that unusually survived the Reformation.

Blessed James of Bitetto

He was the cook at the Abbey of Conversano but nearly everything he prepared was spoiled because he kept falling into ecstasies, levitating, and hovering around the kitchen when he should have been minding the pots and pans. He liked to stare into the fire seeing, on a good day, the spark of God's love and on a bad day, the fires of hell, and was once found with his hands thrust into a big pot of beans into which he was weeping copiously. This became his signature dish and Dukes and Kings came from miles around to taste his Beans Seasoned with Holy Tears. He is the patron saint of molecular gastronomy.

St Notburga

A pious cook in the household of Henry and Ottilia of Rattenberg, she lived in the Tyrol around the turn of the fourteenth century and is the patron saint of knife-throwers. She was so devout she gave the leftovers to the poor rather than to the pigs, as Ottilia commanded her to do. Henry became suspicious and one day ordered a bag search as she left the kitchens, but the food she had taken turned, miraculously, into wood shavings. Ottilia sacked her nevertheless. St Notburga went to work as a farm labourer having first secured a guarantee from her employer that she would be allowed time off to go to Mass. One day, in the thick of the harvest, he insisted she remain in the fields whereupon she threw her sickle over her head and said, 'Let this be the judge between me and you' – it hovered, miraculously, in the air. She went back to work for Henry, for whom things had gone badly wrong since her dismissal. When she died she insisted two oxen decide where to bury her, which they did, at the site of the chapel of St Rupert.

Sts Victorinus, Nicephorus, Dioscorus, Claudian, Victor,

Victorinus and his six martyr companions were all from Corinth, but were banished to Egypt for confessing the faith. There they fell foul of the Governor Sabinus, an enthusiastic persecutor of Christians. At Diospolis in 284 they suffered a unique martyrdom, thrown into a large mortar and pounded with pestles, the executioners starting with their feet and working their way up the body, saying at every stroke: 'Spare yourself, wretch. Renounce your new God!'

Serapion and Papias

It served only to strengthen the resolve of those awaiting their turn, and they leaped of their own accord into the mortar. It got so crowded one had to be burned to death, another beheaded and another thrown into the river.

St Blath of Kildare

She was a lay sister and the cook at St Brigid's convent in Kildare in sixth-century Ireland and considered expert in the logistics of catering. Her portion control was exact, but even if it had not been, her cows, after milking, would miraculously fill up again and provide yet more for the sisters' needs. She is the only person I know of who was canonised for her bacon butties: 'under the care of St Blath, the bread and bacon at St Brigid's table were better than a banquet elsewhere'.

St Barontius

Born in the seventh century, he was a Frankish court official who by his middle years had been married thrice and had taken to himself a great many concubines. One day he fell into a trance and experienced an extraordinary vision. He flew through the air over the city of Bourges attacked by demons until the Archangel Raphael flew alongside and took him on tour of heaven, which was lovely. Demons continued to claw at him, however, in an effort to drag him into hell, so in the end Raphael lost his temper and asked St Peter to come and sort them out. St Peter whacked the demons with his keys and sent them back to hell, but vouchsafed Barontius a tour of its infernal regions and read out a long list of his sins, including some he had forgotten. As a result, Barontius decided to become a hermit with his friend Desiderius, about whom little is known.

St Catherine Labouré

She was the inventor of the Miraculous Medal. Born in France in 1806 she lost her mother when she was a girl, but after the funeral picked up a statue of the Blessed Virgin Mary, said, 'You are my mummy now,' and kissed it. She adored having visions and one day St Vincent de Paul came to her in one and asked if she fancied joining the Daughters of Charity. She did, and not long after the Virgin Mary appeared to her standing on a giant ball wearing gorgeous diamond rings and told her that France was going to the dogs. The globe then rotated, revealing a big 'M' surmounted by a cross and a text appearing to endorse the doctrine of the Immaculate Conception. Mary then asked Catherine if she would kindly arrange to have medallions struck bearing this image. She did and they have proved immensely popular, with millions sold all over the world. She continued prophesying, and sometimes got it right predicting, for example, the assassination of the Archbishop of Paris by the Communards in 1871. Sorry about that. But she was quite often wrong, which led the Republic to dismiss her as 'a silly old thing' and Pope Benedict XIV to observe that sayings derived in rapture are not always reliable.

St Henry of Coquet

He was a hermit of the twelfth century and rather
a dear. Born in Denmark his family wanted him to
marry so he ran away to Coquet Island, off the coast
of Northumberland, to pursue his eremitical vocation.
He grew a little grain and a few berries, and lived a life
of great austerity enjoying it so much that when some
Danes turned up and offered him a lift home he said
no thanks. He prayed in front of a crucifix on which the
figure of Jesus would engage him in conversation from
time to time;word of his holiness soon spread and he
became rather plagued by visitors, to whom he would
point out frightening spectral women gliding in the wake
of doomed ships thereabouts. He once left the island
to see a notoriously drunken monk of Tynemouth to
whom he named the place and hour of his last debauch,
and bargained successfully with demons for the soul
of a priest who had achieved only one good deed in his
wretched life. He also once imposed a penance on a man
for not having sex with his wife in Lent, even though the
man had not mentioned it in Confession.

Eventually he grew old and sick but got more and more
cheerful as death approached. One day the monks
of Tynemouth heard the peal of his hermit's bell,
summoning assistance, but by the time they arrived at
his hermitage he had died, holding the bell rope in one
hand and candle in the other. He then started to glow
with a dazzling whiteness and his cortege got hopelessly
lost in the fog.

St Eustace

The Feast of St Eustace is 20 September; he is the patron saint of hunters. A second-century Roman noble who adored living it up, out hunting one day at Tivoli he was about to despatch a stag when a vision of Jesus appeared between its antlers. Eustace dropped to his knees and immediately converted.

He and his family were baptised and straight away were afflicted with a series of misfortunes to rival those of Job. He lost all his money, his servants died of the plague, his wife was kidnapped, and his two sons were taken by a wolf and a lion. But Eustace remained steadfast in his new faith and his family, wealth and prestige were restored. Unfortunately the emperor then obliged him to make a pagan sacrifice and Eustace refused, so he and his family were roasted to death in a bronze statue of a bull. The Roman Catholic Church, incidentally, describes him as 'absolutely fabulous'.

Blessed Oringa

Oringa of the Holy Cross was born in 1237 to peasant farmers near Lucca and spent much of her lonely childhood looking at cows. Her brothers irked her and when they sought to marry her off she would have none of it and ran away, crossing the swollen Arno miraculously by walking on its turbid waters. In Lucca she found work as a scullery maid. Inspired by St Michael the Archangel she went to Rome, changed her name to Christina, and there met a lady called Margaret who admired her for her piety. They went to visit the tomb of St Francis at Assisi and in a vision Christina was urged to start a convent in her home town. She did, and the sisters became famous for their austerities. She was the most austere of all and fell into an agonising paralysis which she suffered for three years before dying. We are told that during her final illness her face shone with an unearthly light so brightly her sisters could read their prayer books by it.

St Eucherius

He was Bishop of Orléans when the wicked Charles Martel, then mayor of the palace, was looting the Frankish churches to pay for his military adventures. When Eucherius protested, Martel had him exiled to Cologne and thence to Liege where he handed out buns to the poor, After Martel's death, Eucherius was granted a vision of hell wherein he saw him suffering in its sulphurous flames. He went with two friends, Boniface and Fulrad, to Charles' tomb and when they opened it a dragon rushed out of its scorched and blackened interior. Let this be a lesson to those who steal church property, especially to those whoresons who nicked two of our lawnmowers last year.

St Emma

She married Liudger, brother of Benno, Duke of
Saxony, who went to Russia and there caught a peculiar
ague from which he dropped down dead in 1011,
leaving Emma a widow. She retreated to her estates
near Bremen and spent her fortune on its cathedral,
its churches and its poor. One day the townspeople
approached her and asked for a nice meadow. Emma
promised them as much meadow as a man could run
round in an hour and asked the Duke if he would oblige
them with the land. He, mindful of his territories, said
they could have as much as a man could run round in a
day, provided he could pick the man.

Yes, they said, but he picked a legless cripple and
scorned his disappointed sister-in-law with a mocking
laugh. His laughter was silenced, however, when at
Emma's behest the legless cripple rose up and ran like
Pheidippedes all day, encircling an enormous area
of the duke's best land. Hundreds of years after her
death the tomb was opened and it was found her body
had crumbled to dust save the right hand, with which
she had given so generously. She is the patron saint of
paralympians.

St Cosmas and

They were twin brothers and surgeons who practiced in the third-century Roman Empire, and were known as the 'Unmercenary', for they asked no payment for their services. They are best remembered for having grafted a black man's leg onto a white man, one of those rare examples of a miracle anticipating a medical reality. The prefect insisted they recant their faith and they refused so they were crucified, stoned, shot with arrows and finally beheaded.

St Damian

The twins' severed heads have caused controversy, with churches in Munich, Madrid, Syria, Constantinople, Bremen, Rome, Venice, and Vienna all, at some time, claiming to preserve them. They are patrons of surgeons, those seeking husbands, and women wishing to become pregnant. Perhaps for this reason at Naples in the eighteenth century, on their feast day, wax models of penises were presented to them as an offering. Less dramatically, St Damian appears in the arms of the British Dental Association.

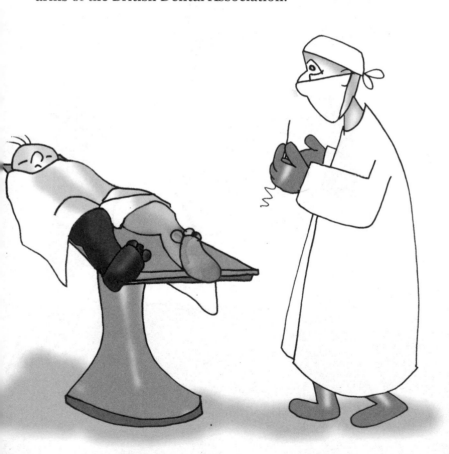

St Catherine of Genoa

She lived in sixteenth-century Italy and made a poor
match with a spendthrift ne'er-do-well. Determined
to win his affection she at first adopted worldly airs,
adapting to what she later described as 'the contagion
of the world's slow stain.' Ten years of this was enough.
She obliged her husband to become a Franciscan
Tertiary, took to her room, coming out only to tend
plague victims, from whom she too contracted the
disease. On her death bed   one of her arms
suddenly grew longer   than the other
and she received the   stigmata, which
wept boiling drops of   blood.

Blessed Isnardo de Chiampo

He was a brilliant Italian friar of the thirteenth century with a tremendous gift for preaching, but unfortunately he was so fat everyone laughed at him and drowned out his sermons. One day a man possessed behaved particularly badly while he was preaching so Isnardo descended the pulpit, gave him a bear hug, and commanded the evil spirit to leave him, which it did. This shut everyone up apart from one sceptical fellow who shouted out, 'I won't believe in fatty unless he makes that barrel over there jump up and hit me'. Immediately, the barrel jumped up and hit the scoffer so hard it broke his leg. Thus Isnardo became the patron saint of those afflicted by hecklers.

Blessed Joscius Roseus of St Bertin

He was a delightful Benedictine monk of the twelfth century who lived near Arras. He so adored saying his Hail Marys that when he died roses grew from his mouth, their petals imprinted with the name of the Blessed Virgin.

St Guthlac

A nobleman and warrior of the kingdom of Mercia, in
699 he renounced his worldly ways and went to pursue
the vocation of a hermit on the island of Crowland, girt
by foul and sucking swamps. There he lived in a mound
of earth, wore animal skins, and lived on a daily diet
of a piece of barley bread and a cup of muddy water.
He had no friends apart from a codfish and a crow
who was a kleptomaniac. He was terribly plagued by
demons, who spoke English but with horribly sibilant
voices and dreadful rough accents, and had 'great
heads, long necks, thin faces, yellow complexions, filthy
beards, shaggy ears, wild foreheads, fierce eyes, foul
mouths, horses' teeth, throats vomiting flames, twisted
jaws, thick lips, strident voices, singed hair, fat cheeks,
pigeons breasts, scabby thighs, knotty knees, crooked
legs, swollen ankles, splay feet, spreading mouths, (and)
raucous cries'. In the end, some angels came to tell
him he was about to die and when he did his soul left
his body through his mouth as a beam of light which
smelled powerfully of nectar and as it made its way to
heaven angels sang. A year later his sister Peg, after a
vision, dug him up and found his shroud glowed in the
dark and filled the island with scent of ambrosia.

St Lidwid of Schiedam

She was born in Holland in the fourteenth century and, aged fifteen, was out skating one day when she fell on her bottom. At first it was thought she had merely winded herself but she began to fall apart and before long whole bits of her dropped off. The bits that were left ceased to function, apart from her left hand. She fasted continuously, living on a piece of apple, a single date and dirty river water, and then renounced sleep. She swelled alarmingly and it was thought she might have got pregnant by the priest sent to her monitor her austerities, but as more bits dropped off, her mother – who kept them in a vase on the mantelpiece – noticed that they gave off a sweet fragrance. The town officials of Schiedam became terribly excited by this and in the end Lidwid had her dropped-off bits buried so as not to excite intrusive attention, but her holiness, marked by ecstasies and visions, made her even more famous and she lived to the age of fifty-three. She is the patron saint of Torville and Dean.

St Job of Pochayiv

A sixteenth-century monk of the Ukraine. He achieved perfection in wisdom by the age of ten and joined the Preobrazhens'kyi Uhornyts'kyi Monastery, where he eventually became the Hegumen. He was a doughty critic of the heresy (as he saw it) of Protestantism, and of Roman Catholic bread-baking. For this he became tremendously famous so withdrew to a cave in the western Ukraine and became a hermit, saying nothing but the Jesus Prayer (Lord Jesus Christ, Son of God, have mercy on me, a sinner). The cave was so small he could neither stand nor sit in it but had to kneel; his knees, which soon streamed with blood, wore two grooves in the rock. He was lit with an unearthly light and became litigious, eventually succeeding in restoring a miracle-working icon to the monastery which had been stolen by Andrzej Firlej, Castellan of Belz. After he died his incorrupt body was found to emit a lovely smell of flowers and he appeared miraculously to fend off various attacks by invading troops (illustrated). In 1759 he also miraculously cured a man of road rage by deflecting the bullets he fired in a fury at his coach driver.

St Juthwara

The only cephalophore to come from Dorset; she is aslo the patron saint of soft cheese. She lived in the sixth century, a pious girl, much given to fasting and prayer. When her father died she was stricken with sorrow and fell prey to heartsickness so her wicked stepmother sent her to bed and applied two soft cheeses to her breasts as a remedy. She then told her son Bana that Juthwara was in fact pregnant. Bana felt her underclothes, found them to be moist, and in a rage chopped off her head. A spring of water miraculously gushed forth at that very spot, and Juthwara picked up her head and walked to the church at Halstock exclaiming pieties. Recently, the church at Halstock dedicated its new extension to St Juthwara, and the Bishop of Sherborne came and gave them a special scroll. There was a pub in the village called The Quiet Woman that was named after her but it closed down.

Blessed Reginald

Blessed Reginald of Saint-Gilles is patron saint of makeovers. He was a lawyer in thirteenth-century France, famed for his eloquence, but filled with zeal for preaching the gospel. He joined the newly formed Dominican order and immediately was stricken with illness. As he lay on his bed St Dominic, who was very taken with him, prayed to Our Lady for succour. His prayers were answered when she, Saint Cecilia and Saint Catherine of Alexandria, appeared at Reginald's bedside holding a lovely white scapular which the Queen of Heaven thought he would look very smart in. She then squirted Reginald with a special fragrance and disappeared. He recovered and was the first to wear the white scapular all Dominicans since have worn. He was also the first to die in one, shortly after, in the Holy Land.

St Hedwig of Silesia

She was High Duchess consort of Poland having married, at the age of twelve, Henry the Bearded who succeeded his father, Bolesław the Tall, in 1201 after a fierce struggle with Mieszko Tanglefoot and Władysław Spindleshanks. Eventually Henry the Bearded overcame all opposition and was made High Duke of Poland in 1231. The High Duchess was very devout, forever founding monasteries and walking around barefoot in winter turning water into wine. She found time to produce an heir, Henry the Pious, whom she later saw slain by Mongols, and Conrad the Curly, who fell off his horse. In 1238 Henry the Bearded died and was buried at Trzebnica Abbey. Hedwig became a nun and was soon famed for her austerities, wearing an iron girdle, sleeping on the floor, starving herself to the point of emaciation and scourging herself until she bled profusely. She also adored kissing the sores of the afflicted which may have contributed to her death at Trzebnica in 1243. She gave her name to a range of luxury glassware, fourteen examples of which survive. She is patron saint of victims of jealousy.

St Ignatius of Antioch

He was one of the five Apostolic Fathers. He lived in the second century and had been a pupil of the disciple St John. He coined the word 'Catholic' and also, accidentally, invented bishops. He was eaten by lions, which became rather the vogue. Not to be confused with Pseudo-Ignatius.

St Erkenwald of London

He was a Saxon of the blood royal who founded a monastery at Chertsey in Surrey and a convent at Barking, where he installed his sister Ethelburga as abbess. In 675 he was consecrated Bishop of London by St Theodore of Canterbury but sat on a sofa all day on account of a terrible gouty toe. This got so bad he was carried around on it. After he died, the sofa was discovered to have the miraculous property of healing gout and was much in demand until it was chopped up and burned during the Reformation. There was a charming poem about him, written in the fourteenth century. In it, St Erkenwald rather charmingly weeps over a zombie which amounts to a baptism and the zombie immediately crumbles into dust releasing its tormented soul to bliss. More bishops should do this sort of thing, we feel. The opening is shown opposite:

At London in England not full long sythen,
Sythen Crist suffrid on crosse and Cristendome stablyd,
Ther was a byschop in þat burgh, blessyd and sacryd;
Saynt Erkenwolde as I hope þat holy mon hatte.
In his tyme in þat toun þe temple alder-grattyst
Was drawen doun, þat one dole, to dedifie new,
For hit hethen had bene in Hengyst dawes

St Felix of Dunwich

The Apostle of the East Angles was a seventh-century Burgundian missionary who wrought the conversion of Sigebert and was sent by St Honorius of Canterbury to the Suffolk seaside as a reward. There he founded his See at Dunwich, and toiled for 20 years converting the pagan folk who lived along the route of the A14 and A11. He established a famous boys' school which some have proposed, without foundation, as the foundation of the University of Cambridge. When he died his body was taken to Soham Abbey, to which the felonious monks of Ramsey and of Ely raced during the reign of Cnut. Ramsey won, bashed up the monks of Soham and snatched the decayed body of St Felix, making their escape in a boat under the cover of fog.

Dunwich still has a bishop, Clive, a Suffragan of St Edmundsbury and Ipswich, but the town itself was swept into the sea in the St Lucia's Flood of 1287. It is said that during a storm the bells of its drowned churches may be heard tolling beneath the waves. I once put this to the test with the well-known actress Tilda Swinton but in the end we gave up and went for a restorative at the Ship Inn instead.

St Odile

She was born blind, a daughter of Aldaric, Duke of
Alsace in the year 660. He was so displeased to have
sired a blind child, and – worse – a girl, he had her sent
away to be raised by peasants. When she was twelve,
an angel led a passing bishop to where she lived. He
baptised her and her sight was miraculously restored.
Her brother came to fetch her home but when they
arrived her father was so displeased to see her he killed
his son in a rage. Odile raised her brother from the
dead but not wanting to cause a fuss, went away again.
Her father still raging, pursued her, so a mountain
miraculously opened up and she hid in it while rocks
rained down until her father went away. Years later
they were reconciled and she founded a convent with
a miraculous well that could cure blindness. She was
much loved by her sisters, so much so that
when she died they all prayed for her to
come back to life. She did, but crossly
told them she was quite enjoying
heaven and would they please
not disturb her. She received
communion and died again.

St Marinus

The founder of the world's oldest republic, he was a Croatian stonemason who fled the island of Rab during the persecution of the Emperor Diocletian and arrived in Rimini, where he was ordained deacon. His ecclesiastical career, unfortunately, stalled when a mad woman wrongly identified him as her husband and insisted on both conjugal rights and help around the house, so he fled again and became a hermit on Monte Titano.

He founded a monastery there and when he died in in the year 366 his last words to his brethren were, 'Relinquo vos liberos ab utroque homine,' (I leave you free from both men) referring to both the Emperor and the Pope. Ever since, San Marino – as it is now known – has enjoyed a robust and picturesque independence. Being so tiny, it has a poor record in international sport, lying 203rd out of 203 in the FIFA football rankings and holding the record for the worst result in the European Championships, losing 13–0 to Germany in 2006. It also came last in its first attempt at the Eurovision Song Contest, but this year, returning to the fray, did rather better when Valentina Monetta, singing 'The Social Network Song', achieved fourteenth place.

St Sabbas the Sanctified

He was born in Cappadocia in the fifth century and entered a monastery at the age of eight where his piety was very quickly noticed. Offered an apple he remarked that it was through this fruit that sin came into the world, and stamped it to pulp under his sandaled foot. To this day his followers will not eat apples. Aged seventeen he was tonsured and received the charism of thaumaturgy. He practiced this by causing wells to spring up before moving on to more difficult miracles like banishing demons. After ten years in the monastery he got so fed up with the squabbling of the monks he went to live in a cave, but had to persuade a lion who was living there to move out first. Word got out that he had been eaten by the lion which caused another tremendous squabble in the monastery until he turned up to show that he was still alive. In the end he went

off into the wilderness where he wove baskets from willow, but managed to muster a following of 10,000 monks to resist the threat of monophysitism. He is patron saint of occupational therapists.

St Cuthmann of Steyning

He was born in Cornwall in the seventh century and became a shepherd on the moors. He liked to wander off and sit on a rock, so would trace a miraculous circle in the gorse beyond which his sheep never strayed. Tiring of the harsh Cornish weather, however, he decided to move east, so he put his mother in a wheelbarrow and got as far as Steyning in West Sussex when the wheelbarrow broke. He decided it was God's will that he should stop there and build a church. He put his mother in a hut and started work on a church, much to the amusement of two local youths, who stole his oxen. Cuthmann miraculously yoked them to his cart and work continued. Having built the church he became so successful an evangelist that the devil grew angry and decided one night to dig a channel to the sea to drown the new Christians of Sussex. Cuthmann learned of his plan and used a candle and a cock to trick the devil into thinking it was dawn and he fled, leaving behind the complex of earthworks known as Chanctonbury Ring. For this, Cuthmann is the patron saint of the Environment Agency.

St Godfrey

Dear St Godfrey was a sweetheart. Raised by monks in Soissons in the eleventh century he was made abbot of the most dilapidated monastery in all Christendom, where the monks were few and hopeless. He did such a good job of turning it round he was offered the famous Abbey of Saint-Remi, but refused, saying, 'God forbid I should ever desert a poor bride by preferring a rich one'. He once broke a drought by getting sheep and ducks to fast and caused pelting rain to fall on everyone, which annoyed them. Unfortunately the bishopric of Amiens was forced upon him in 1104, but he annoyed the people there by continuing to live simply, giving away a delicious salmon specially prepared for him to the poor, insisting his clergy turn up for services and put away their concubines, one of whom, it is recorded, grew 'disgruntled'. It is unwise to disgruntle a clergyman's concubine and everyone turned on him so he ran away to the great monastery at Grande-Chartreuse, there to live in silence and solitude. Unfortunately the people who had driven him away had a change of heart once he'd gone and insisted he return, so he went to see the archbishop to complain, but died on the way. For some reason, in art he is often shown with a dead dog at his feet.

St Marguerite d'Youville

Foundress of the Grey Nuns of Montreal, she was born in 1701 in Quebec. In her teens she was seen as something of a catch in Quebecois society. Unfortunately, in widowhood, her mother dallied with an Irish doctor and was rather ostracised by polite society, so Marguerite ended up marrying a ne'er-do-well who became a bootlegger, trading alcohol for furs with the Native Americans thereabouts. He soon died and Marguerite, who experienced a religious ecstasy, devoted the rest of her life to the care of the poor and destitute. She began by cutting down and burying the bodies of those hanged on the public gallows, treating the syphilitic and, most scandalous, feeding the hungry, which she funded by making and selling lingerie. In spite of the profound disapprobation of society she was joined in this enterprise by a group of women and so she founded a religious order known as the Grey Sisters, not because of the habit they wore but because the outraged Quebecois accused them of being drunk and disorderly. In Quebec someone who is completely pissed is said to be 'Grise'. She was tremendously fond, all her life, of singing and dancing, which may have raised the suspicions of her sober-sided neighbours. We, however, adore her.

St Abraham of Smolensk

A stern and austere monk of the Bogoroditzkaja
monastery he scared everyone with terrifying sermons
about the Last Judgment and enraged the wealthy by
denouncing the emptiness of worldly riches. Irritating
his brethren, he was moved to the monastery of the
Holy Cross which he gave a make-over and worked
tirelessly with the sick and the poor. For this he was
particularly disliked by his fellow clergy who brought
against him trumped-up charges of philandering and
reading naughty books, and insisted he be drowned
or burned. The bishop found against him and he was
censured, but this caused a drought which lasted for
five years. Eventually the bishop relented, acquitted
Abraham, and immediately it began to rain. He was
then sent to be abbot of the monastery of the Placing of
the Robe of the Most Holy Mother of God, but was so
strict and gloomy only seventeen monks managed to
put up with him. He died peacefully in 1221.

St Aidan of Ferns

A sixth-century Irish saint, he was a favourite of St David of Wales who taught him in his monastery at Menevia. He was a swotty lad, but one day left a book he was reading on the beach which was lost to the incoming tide. St David made him prostrate himself at the same spot as a penance but then forgot about him and it was only later that evening he was discovered, still prostrated, underwater but miraculously alive. The other monks grew jealous of David's affection for Aidan and one tried to kill him, but David, in a vision, saw him raise the axe to strike the fatal blow and miraculously stayed the assassin's hand. His murderous arm was thereafter forever raised, which must have been annoying. St David died in Aidan's arms and he went back to Ireland where he became a great softie, giving his food away to the poor and living on barley bread and water for seven years. He was particularly kind to animals. When he came across a stag being pursued by hounds he made it invisible and it escaped. However, he could be stern. Coming across some fake beggars Aidan tore the clothes from their backs to give to the poor and sent them away naked. When he died he bequeathed his bell to the MacGovern family of Templeport, who have loaned it to the Library in Armagh.

St Julian of Antioch

He was a noble Christian during the reign of the Emperor Diocletian and was arrested during his notorious persecution of Christians. For this he suffered swingeing tortures and was paraded round his hometown daily before finally suffering the unusual martyrdom of being sewn up in a sack half-filled with scorpions and vipers and thrown into the sea.

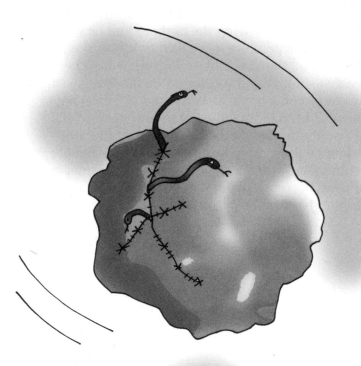

St Guy

He was known as 'The Poor Man of Anderlecht'. Born in the tenth century to pious peasants he showed early signs of an extraordinary detachment from worldly possessions, working as a farm labourer but assisted at the plough by some helpful angels. For this reason he was appointed sacristan of the church of Our Lady at Laeken. Unfortunately, in the expectation that he would become rich and then give it all away, he decided to invest in a shipping venture, but the boat immediately sank on leaving the harbour and he was left destitute. As a penance he walked to Rome, then to Jerusalem and then back to Anderlecht, where he died of exhaustion. His grave, forgotten for years, was rediscovered when a horse kicked it and two local boys, who ridiculed his memory, died of tummy ache. Well into the twentieth century the cab drivers of Brabant held an annual pilgrimage to Anderlecht in his honour which culminated with a carthorse race. The winner got a hat of roses presented by the parish priest. The Poor Man of Anderlecht is the patron saint of sheds.

A Calendar of
IMPRoBABLE
and UNLIKELY
SAINTS

With some additional odd, intriguing
and obscurely relevant anniversaries

'Ora pro nobis!'

January

1   New Year's Day
2   Brigham Young, leader of the Mormons arrested on a charge of bigamy. He had 25 wives (1872)
3   St Hieromartyr Theopompus
4   Blessed Oringa of the Holy Cross
5   St Simeon the Stylite
6   Epiphany
7   Old Christmas
8   Vikings attacked Lindisfarne (794)
9   UK income tax introduced at 2d in the £ (1799)
10 St Marcian of Constantinople, patron saint of strippers
11 St Vitalis of Gaza
12 St Arcadius of Mauretania
13 Thomas Crapper pioneers flushing lavatory (1863)
14 St Hilary, giving name to winter university term
15 The Eve of St Ita
16 St Sulpicius the Débonnaire
17 Captain Scott reaches South Pole ... second (1912)
18 St Prisca
19 St Fillan of Munster, patron saint of mentally ill
20 St Sebastian
21 St Agnes
22 Blessed Guillaume-Joseph Chaminade
23 St Eusebius of Mount Coryphe
24 St Cadoc
25 St Dwynwen of Angelsey
26 St Paula, patron saint of widows
27 St Devota, patron saint of Monaco
28 St Thomas Aquinas
29 Inaugurations of the Victoria Cross (1856)
30 St Balthild of Ascania
31 St Aidan of Ferns

February

1   Blessed Reginald of Saint-Gilles, patron saint of makeovers
2   Candlemas
3   St Blaise, patron saint of sore throats
4   St Veronica
5   St Agatha, patron saints of bell ringers and more
6   St Mel
7   St Luke the Wonder Worker
8   St Cuthmann of Steyning
9   Bishop of Gloucester burned at the stake (1555)
10   St Paul shipwrecked at Malta (60)
11   Appearance of Our Lady of Lourdes (1858)

12   Alexander Selkirk, the original Robinson Crusoe, rescued after four years on Fernandez Island (1709)
13   St Martinian the Hermit
14   Sts Valentine of Terni and Valentine of Rome
15   St Sigfrid, patron saint of Sweden
16   St Onesimus
17   St Colmán eve, patron saint of those who sulk
18   St Flavian of Constantinople
19   St Conrad of Piacenza
20   St Eucherius

21   Blessed Noel Pinot, patron saint of the properly dressed
22   St Margaret of Cortona, patron saint of floozies
23   St Serenus the Gardener, the patron saint of those who suffer imaginary slights
24   St Matthias, the apostle chosen by lot
25   Sts Victorinus, Victor, Nicephorus et al
26   St Isabelle of France, patron saint of precocious children
27   St Gabriel of Our Lady of Sorrows
28   St Oswald of Worcester, Archbishop of York
29   Leap years only

March

1 St Giovanna Marie Bonomo
2 Blessed Charles the Good murdered (1127)
3 St Cunigunde of Luxembourg
4 St Adrian of Nicomedia
5 St Kieran
6 St Fridolin, the Irish Wanderer
7 St Paul the Simple
8 St Felix of Dunwich, apostle of the East Angles
9 St Frances of Rome
10 Blessed Peter de Geremia, patron of penitent lawyers
11 St Aurea the Anchoress
12 St Fina of San Gimignano
13 Sts Roderick and Solomon
14 St Matilda of Saxony
15 St Longinus the Centurion
16 St Julian of Antioch
17 St Joseph of Arimathea
18 St Edward, king and martyr
19 Blessed Clement of Dunblane
20 Blessed Maurice of Hungary
21 St Enda of Aranmore
22 Blessed Isnardo de Chiampo, the patron of those afflicted by hecklers
23 Sts Gwinear, Phiala and companions
24 Death of the Virgin Queen, Elizabeth 1 (1603)
25 St Barontius, hermit of Pistoia
26 St Basil the Younger
27 St Amador of Portugal, invoked against aphids
28 Good King Guntram
29 St Woolos the Bearded
30 St John of the Ladder
31 St Jacqueline, patron saint of forgetfulness

April

1 St Catalina of Palma
2 St Francis of Paola, patron saint of vegans
3 St Richard of Chichester
4 Zosimas of Palestine
5 St Derfel
6 St Brychan
7 St Hermann Joseph
8 St Constance
9 St Waltrude of Mons
10 St Bademus of Persia
11 St Guthlac
12 St Tetricus
13 Blessed Margaret of Metola
14 St Lidwid of Schiedam
15 St Padarn
16 St Benedict Labre, patron saint of the victims of
   unjust housing policies
17 Blessed Thora of Pisa
18 St Idesbald of the Dunes
19 St Emma
20 St Hildegund, the patron saint of trousers
21 Sts Simeon Barsabae and Companions
22 St Theodore of Sykeon
23 Toyohiko Kagawa
24 St William Firmatus, patron saint of headaches
25 St Macaille of Croghan
26 Our Lady of Good Counsel
27 Blessed James of Bitetto, patron saint of
   molecular gastronomy
28 Sts Patricius, Acatius, Menander and Polyenus
29 St Catherine of Siena
30 St Erkenwald of London

May

1 Hildebrand of Fossombrone
2 St Waldebert
3 The discovery of the True Cross (335)
4 St Monica, mother of St Augustine of Hippo
5 Second Council of Constantinople opens (553)
6 St Dominic Savio
7 Evita – Eva Perón's birthday (1919)
8 St Arsenius the Great
9 St Bienheuré
10 St Solange
11 St Anthony of St Ann Galvão
12 St Dominic of the Causeway
13 Roman Pantheon turned into a church (609)
14 Sts Victor and Corona. Corona is the patron saint of the tooth fairy
15 Isidore the Farmer, patron saint of peasants
16 St Aaron
17 San Pascualito Muerte, King of the Graveyard
18 St Eric
19 Anne Boleyn beheaded (1536)
20 St Abercius
21 St Helena
22 St Quiteria, patron saint for the rabid
23 St Desiderius of Vienne
24 St Sara the Black, patron of gypsies
25 St Philip Neri died (1595)
26 St Augustine of Canterbury died (604)
27 Thirty Hungarian jews burned at stake after notorious blood libel trial (1529)
28 St Bernard of Menthon, patron saint of snowboarders
29 Charles II restored to the English throne
30 St Joan of Arc
31 St Petronella, patron saint of dolphins

June

1   St Ronan
2   Coronation of Queen Elizabeth II (1953)
3   Pope John XXIII died (1963)
4   St Saturnina
5   St Boniface
6   St Norbert, patron saint of bohemians
7   St Robert of Newminster
8   St Medard, patron saint of toothache sufferers
9   St Columba died (597)
10   St Landry of Paris
11   The Feast of St Barnabas
12   St Humphrey, patron saint of those seeking lost
      articles
13   St Anthony of Padua
14   St Methodius of Constantinople
15   St Germaine Cousin, patron saint of losers
16   St Benno, patron saint of alliteration
17   St Herve, patron saint of horse vets
18   St Elizabeth of Schönau
19   St Juliana Falconieri, patron saint of nausea
20   Blessed Margareta Ebner
21   St Aloysius Gonzaga
22   St Eusebius of Samosata
23   St Audrey
24   Lucrezia Borgia, notorious daughter of Pope
      Alexander VI dies (1519)
25   St William of Montevergine
26   St Josemaría Escrivá
27   St John of Chinon
28   St Vitus
29   Thomas Cromwell, destroyer of the English
      monasteries, sentenced to death as heretic (1540)
30   St Martial

July

1   Sir Thomas More stands trial for treason (1535)
2   Sts Martinius and Processus
3   St Phocas, patron saint of gardeners
4   Oda the Severe, patron saint of Wimbledon
5   St Zoe of Rome
6   St Goar of Aquitaine, patron saint of potters
7   St Maolruain of Tallaght
8   St Theophilus the Myrrh-gusher
9   St Veronica Giuliani
10   The Seven Brothers
11   St Benedict, Patron of Europe
12   Day of Devotion to Veronica's Face of Jesus
13   St Teresa of the Andes
14   St Francis Solanus
15   St Swithun
16   St Helier
17   St Kenelm
18   St Arnold, patron of brewers
19   Sts Justa and Rufina
20   St Wilgefortis
21   St Victor of Marseilles
22   St Markella
23   St Birgitta of Sweden died (1373)
24   Abdication of Mary Queen of Scots (1567)
25   St James, the apostle
26   St Anne, grandmother of Jesus
27   The Seven Sleepers of Ephesus
28   St Alphonsa of the Immaculate Conception
29   St Martha of Bethany
30   St Leopold Mandic died (1942)
31   St Germanus of Auxerre

August

1   St Abgar the Black
2   St Basil
3   St Waltheof
4   St Sithney
5   St Oswald
6   St Jocelin
7   St Donatus of Arezzo
8   St Mary McKillop
9   St Herman of Alaska
10   St Bessus
11   St Fiacre, patron saint of piles, cabbies and more
12   Cleopatra dies from an asp bite (30 BC)
13   St Cassian of Imola
14   St Athanasia of Constantinople
15   Macbeth becomes King of Scots (1040)
16   St Rock, patron saint of dogs
17   St Clare of the Cross
18   Sts Floridus and Laurus, patron saint of home improvements
19   Five 'witches' executed in Salem, Massachusetts (1692)
20   St Amadour
21   St Abraham of Smolensk
22   St Andrew the Scot
23   St Rose of Lima, patron saint of Peru, florists and arguing families
24   St Eutychius of Phrygia
25   Council of Nicaea ends endorsing The Trinity (325)
26   St Irenaeus drowned in Roman sewer (258)
27   Transverberation of the heart of Teresa of Avila
28   USA's oldest city founded, St Augustine, Florida (1565)
29   Anti-Pope Callistus III resigns (1178)
30   Margaret Clitherow
31   Death of Diana, Princess of Wales, acclaimed a secular saint (1997)

September

1   Destruction of Jerusalem (69)
2   St Nonnosus
3   St Marinus
4   Pope St Boniface I died (422)
5   Peter the Great imposes a tax on beards (1698)
6   Maya Long Count Calendar started (3114 BC)
7   Pretender Perkin Warbeck proclaimed English King Richard IV (1497)
8   St Genebald
9   Pope St Sergius I died (701) as Catholic Pope
10   St Hyacinth
11   St Pratt
12   St Guy, the patron saint of sheds
13   St John the Golden-Mouthed
14   St Notburga, the patron saint of knife-throwers
15   St Catherine of Genoa
16   St Edith of Wilton
17   St Lambert
18   St Joseph of Cupertino, died (1663)
19   St Januarius
20   National Punch Day
21   King Richard the Lionheart captured (1192)
22   Saint Emmeram of Regensburg
23   St Padre Pio
24   Feast of Our Lady Of Walsingham,
25   St Cleopas, who met Jesus on the Emmaus road
26   Sts Cosmas and Damian
27   Pope Urban VII dies (1590)– the shortest papacy in history (13 days)
28   St Wenceslas murdered by his brother (935)
29   St Rhipsime
30   St Jerome

October

1   Blessed Edward James, martyred (1588)

2   St Leger

3   Dafydd ap Gruffyd, first nobleman to be hung, drawn and quartered (1283)

4   First complete Bible in English printed (1537)

5   St Pelagia the Harlot

6   St Foy

7   Sts Sergius and Bacchus

8   Blessed Ambrose Sansedoni of Siena

9   St Denis

10 St Cerbonius

11 St Kenny

12 St Wilfrid of Ripon

13 Nero's reign of terror and persecution begins (54)

14 St Hedwig of Silesia, patron saint of victims of jealousy

15 The burning of Bishops Latimer and Ridley (1555)

16 St Marguerite d'Youville

17 St Richard Gwyn

18 St Justus of Beauvais

19 St Jean de Brébeuf

20 St Acca of Hexham

21 St Hilarion

22 St Donagh of Fiesole

23 St John of Capistrano

24 Dedication of Chartres Cathedral (1260)

25 St Marcius the Hermit

26 St Demetrius the Myrrh-Streamer

27 Constantine the Great sees vision of the cross (312)

28 St Job of Pochayiv

29 Sir Walter Raleigh beheaded (1618)

30 Thousands taken in by Orson Welles' broadcast of *War of the Worlds* (1938)

31 All Hallows' Eve

November

1   All Saints' Day
2   All Souls' Day
3   Henry VIII becomes Supreme Head of
    Church of England (1534)
4   Mischief Night
5   Bonfire Night
6   Abraham Lincoln elected President of USA (1860)
7   Engelbert, Saint and Archbishop, murdered (1225)
8   St Godfrey
9   St Benen of Armagh
10 Martin Luther, born (1483)
11 Martinus, Bishop of Tours, dies (397)
12 St Renatus of Angers
13 St Augustine of Hippo born (354)
14 St Malo's Eve
15 St Albert the Great
16 St Gertrude the Great
17 St Hugh of Lincoln
18 St Juthwara
19 St Hilary becomes Pope (461)
20 St Edmund
21 St Albert of Louvain
22 St Cecilia
23 English parliament expels Jesuits and Catholic
    priests (1584)
24 Baruch de Spinoza, philosopher born (1632)
25 Isaac Watts, hymn writer, dies (1748)
26 St Katharine Drexel, born (1858)
27 Pope Urban II orders 1st Crusade, (1095)
28 Saint Catherine Labouré
29 St Saturnine
30 Blessed Joscius Roseus of St Bertin

December

1   St Eloi, patron saint of numismatists
2   St Vivian, patron saint of hangovers
3   St Cassian of Tangiers, patron saint of
    stenographers
4   St Barbara, patron saint of artillerymen,
    Australian miners and metallurgists
5   St Sabbas the Sanctified
6   St Nicholas
7   St Ambrose, patron saint of beekeepers, geese
    and the French army's logistical corps
8   Immaculate Conception
9   San Juan Diego
10 St Eulalia
11 St Daniel of Constantinople
12 St Bugga
13 St Lucia
14 St Spyridon, patron saint of Tolstoy family
15 Napoleon interred in Paris (1840)
16 St Adelaide of Italy
17 Lord of Misrule
18 Charles Wesley born (1707)
19 St Anastasius I
20 European powers first recognise Belgium (1830)
21 Winter Solstice
22 St Francesca Xavier Cabrini
23 The Night of the Radishes, Mexico
24 Christmas Eve
25 Christmas Day
26 St Stephen
27 Sts Theodore and Theophanes
28 Holy Innocents
29 St Thomas Becket (1170)
30 Wearing masks at balls forbidden in Boston (1809)
31 Hogmanay